PERSONAL FINANCE FOR TEENS AND COLLEGE STUDENTS

101 MONEY SECRETS YOU WISH YOU LEARNED IN HIGH SCHOOL

JULIAN PAUL

CONTENTS

Introduction   vii

1. The First Money Villain   1
2. What If I Just Make More Money?   21
3. The Most Silent of All Money Stealers   31
4. The Casino's Advantage   51
5. "Your Product Sucks" Says the Agent   60
6. Defeating The First Villain   74
7. Slaying The Tax Dragon   99
8. The Inflation Assassination   109
9. Buy, Borrow, And Then You Die   130

Conclusion   149
References   153
Image Credits   163

This book is dedicated to my mother Theresa.
We're still trying to figure out how she raised five successful children
by herself.

Just For You!

A Gift To Our Readers

101+ Money Secrets that you can
download and put to use right away.
Visit this link:

www.101MoneySecrets.com

INTRODUCTION

Personal finance is intimately connected to your life in almost every way you can imagine.

From the time you are born (and the months leading up to birth) until the day you die (and months after death), personal finance will be right there, every step of the way.

How you handle money and your personal finances can lead to a life filled with more ease and comfort, or a life subject to more worry and stress.

There's good news and bad news when it comes to money...

Let's start with the bad news first.

The bad news—it's pretty easy to mismanage money, especially when you're new to the game.

Why is it so easy to mismanage money?

Because the game of money is set up for you to fail. Plain and simple.

Every time you earn a little slice of money, you get taxed on the money you earn, so you have less of it. Then, when you go to spend the (less) money you just earned, you're taxed again at the register, so now you have to spend a larger amount of that (less) money – which means you have even less!

But even if you do nothing and just keep the money saved, you still lose over time because the costs of goods and services continue to rise, and inflation devalues your money the longer you hold it.

If you thought that was it, you're sorely mistaken.

It's only half the story because you still have to navigate the financial hurdles we're all faced with, such as shady investments, unscrupulous loved ones, and unexpected emergencies—each of which can cause you to lose or give up large chunks of money at once. There are no educational courses that can help us avoid all of these pitfalls.

To top it all off, we learn very little, if anything, about personal finance in school, so our primary source of guidance on the topic comes from parents, pop culture, and the big banks.

The issue with these sources of guidance stems from three areas:

1. The big banks are corporations designed to profit off of us;
2. Pop culture loves drama and typically glamorizes the negative side of money; and,
3. If your parents were like mine, money was never really discussed at length.

Speaking of parents, this reminds me of my upbringing.

My sweet mother did the best she could raising the five of us herself, and the idea of personal finance for our household was a prayer to the heavens when the money ran dry with a week or two left before the next payday.

In my childhood, we never had any fireside chats about money ("Tonight kids, we're going to have a discussion about personal finance and all the money we don't have...").

Nope. Not even once.

This is the situation we're all up against when dealing with personal finance.

"This all sounds terrible! I thought there was good news?!" I know you're thinking.

Don't worry, there IS good news!

The good news is that the steps to take for you to have a financial life filled with ease and comfort are actually quite simple.

However, just because it's simple doesn't mean it's easy.

There is a certain mindset that you have to develop. Also, the younger you are, the quicker it will be for you to pave this path to financial peace of mind.

But whatever age you are, today is the youngest you will ever be, so there's no better time to start paving your path than today.

It's fantastic that you've got your hands on this book. This book will give you an unconventional approach to finance, and I encourage you to continue finding knowledge that's outside the norm.

In my life, I spent five years getting very formal training as a financial professional and built a solid book of clients. Even still, the best training I received was after I walked away from the multi-billion dollar industry and started learning on my own from confidential, private teachers who had very small followings.

SPOILER ALERT

Allow me to apologize in advance, for this book is not all butterflies and rainbows.

Some parts of this book may give you the sensation of being awakened from a sound sleep at 4am by a bucket of ice water.

Just imagine it's your guardian angel with the bucket of water – and there's a nightmare you've been dying to wake up from.

If you couldn't tell, this isn't your father's "Rich Dad Poor Dad" financial book.

For some of you, you make think you already know what this book's all about.

This book is unlike anything you've ever read on the subject of personal finance.

Many books out there try to get you to believe the key to keeping your finances in check is "saving money". Or maybe you've learned the key to personal finance is "investing".

If it were that easy, how come the majority of people still live in financial distress?

Why do most schoolteachers, firefighters, doctors, lawyers, professors, financial advisors, celebrities, and star athletes still worry about not having enough money?

There is not one financial expert or investor who can claim they have never made horrible mistakes with their money. Only after they undergo a few economic downfalls do they learn the tricks and become more competent than those around them.

The more you experiment with new ideas, fail, learn from your mistakes, and rise again, the more confidence you'll gain.

That being said, you don't have to repeat the same mistakes.

This book will explore the foundational aspects of the money game and show you how to navigate the common pitfalls (a.k.a. money villains) that keep you caged in the traditional 9–5, "work until 65" mentality. You'll know how to break free from outdated financial norms and ideas that aren't relevant today.

But the only way you can learn to navigate the pitfalls is for you first to understand what these pitfalls are. We will bring these "money demons" into the light, so you can better understand them and learn how to deal with them if you ever face them.

The first part of this book may be rough for the tender-hearted. Still, it is essential that you have the right mindset so you can take full advantage of the strategies to conquer personal finance and separate yourself from the everyday struggles you will encounter.

If you are working with a loved one you trust (parent, sibling, romantic partner, best friend, etc.), you will have an advantage over someone who has to figure this all out on their own. So if you are by yourself right now, it's strongly encouraged that you find a partner you trust who is willing to go on this journey with you.

Money can be a force for you if you know how to channel its energy in the right direction.

I hope you make the most of this book and use it as a stepping stone into your successful wealth creation experience.

You will never think about money the same way after you finish this book.

Quote me on it.

So, let's get started!

CHAPTER 1
THE FIRST MONEY VILLAIN

"Take time to deliberate; but when the time for action arrives, stop thinking and go in."

— ANDREW JACKSON

L et's get this out of the way right now... In the game of money, the cards are stacked against you.

Most of us are playing the game on the hardest level, and haven't yet learned the rules of the game.

Most of us owe more debt than we have savings. And very few are certain of where they're headed financially, or if/when they're going to finally win the money game so they don't have to play anymore.

Whether it's our parents, the baby boomers' generation, the millennials, or generation Z, everyone is in the same boat when it comes to their understanding of the money game.

To play well and win the money game, you need to be acquainted with the playing field and know who is against you. If you continue to heed the trite advice that doing well in academia and having a job is enough, you'll perhaps never win at this game.

GONE ARE THE DAYS WHEN PEOPLE COULD RELY ON THEIR JOBS, careers, salaries, and promotions. In the past, perhaps it was more common to retire at a certain age and enjoy a decent standard of living.

Our grandparents had it easy. They lived with a particular mindset that worked for them to an extent. They enjoyed modest thrills and modest worries.

They never thought of anything beyond the conventional career path because their lives were simpler. Television was a brand new thing. There was no internet or social media. There were no cell phones. Consumerism wasn't in full swing yet. Student loans were a brand new concept. Life was much less complicated back then!

It's a radically different world of finance that we live in today.

If you don't have a modern financial blueprint to depend on, you'll always be wondering how to save more money, how to get a raise on the paycheck you draw each month, and how to pay off your student loans, credit cards, and other debts faster.

THE CONVENTIONAL CAREER PATH

The traditional idea of working a delightful job, earning a handsome salary, paying off a hefty mortgage, and building a bountiful retirement savings is no longer practical for the everyday person.

To begin with, most people aren't satisfied with their job in this current age.

Employees and employers seem to have become robots who have lost touch with their authentic selves. This happens due to habitually being in demeaning or disempowering situations while wishing to be somewhere else, doing something different.

However, we're taught that if you want to draw a hefty paycheck, you must be part of the mad rat race that doesn't give you a moment to breathe.

Besides, climbing the corporate ladder is difficult, as there's fierce competition and little guidance on navigating corporate politics and entry-level challenges.

While digitalization has created many opportunities, it has also reduced or replaced some careers. It's an era of digital innovators and entrepreneurs.

If you can conceive and build a novel idea and convert it into a money-making prospect, you can do wonders with your career. You'll probably not need to depend on a day job to make ends meet and cultivate a nest egg.

However, many workers are wary of escaping the security of their 9-5 job to jump into an opportunity they're unfamiliar with. It is also challenging to go into business as an entrepreneur with no guarantee of success.

People stick to their jobs because they have certain necessary expenses (rent, food, and transportation) to take care of.

The fear of dabbling in another career and failing is an understandable concern. Most would vastly prefer to stick with something stable and secure that's already there rather than venture into places that are unknown adventures.

Unfortunately, the 9-5 grind can wear down a person so much that they have no energy to devote to another business or side hustle.

If you are working a job right now, you need to come to terms with the glaring fact that the wages you are paid will not keep up with the pace of inflation and the rising costs of living.

For example, college tuition has increased eight times faster than wages since 1988. Wedding costs have increased by 370% since the 1970s. And median home prices have increased 20x since the 1950s. Mortgages that used to cost $50/month in 1950 now cost $800+/month.[1]

Let me ask you this question. This is a serious question.

Which job can you think of right now that's experienced a 20x increase in wages since 1950?

Think about it. I'll wait.

Median wages in the 1950s were $3,300, and median wages in 2020 were about $40,000, which is only a 15x increase. However, we have even more things to buy today compared to the things they had to buy back then. And *everything* is increasing in cost.[2]

This is why most young professionals will remain stuck in the nine-to-five rut, and are unlikely to explore additional income streams.

While many people today are experimenting with multiple income options and remain open to unconventional opportunities, a significant percentage of people live with unrealistic expectations.

They believe they're going to survive economic calamities, pay off their debt, and live a comfortable life after retirement with the job they have, simply by using social security and whatever savings they've managed to retain.

The reality of the situation is not as straightforward as we've hoped it to be.[3]

MONEY TALK AMONGST COLLEGE STUDENTS

Financial literacy is a major solution to the cluelessness and uncertainty that we have in our young minds after graduating high school and going through college.

Specific financial knowledge can give you the true picture of the entire economic scenario of the world and how to find your footing in it.

Unfortunately, most young students avoid discussing money because it has become synonymous with debt.[4]

In college, when students discuss money, they typically talk about their college expenses, student loans, credit cards, and other bills.

However, the percentage of students who talk about the need for budgeting, saving for emergencies, and investing is still not very high, which is apparently due to the lack of financial education.

In today's times, only ten states in the U.S. require financial literacy courses for high school students, and no colleges require a financial literacy course for graduation. In fact, the majority of students don't even know if their college offers financial literacy programs or not.[4]

Whether it's high school or college, the focus for students is mainly on studying random subject matter you won't remember, cramming for exams, and scoring high grades.

Doesn't it seem rational that schools would teach just basic personal finance lessons, such as the use of a savings account or how to manage discretionary expenses?

What a dream that would be!

Sadly, when you are not exposed to how money works early on in life, it's more likely you will inadvertently make reckless financial decisions and be completely unaware of the long-term impact.

Debt becomes an all-too-common reality for many of us, and we get caught up in a vicious cycle of trying to figure out how to "make ends meet".

This thirst for financial knowledge starts when we're quite young.

According to a recent study, 8 out of 10 students in college get anxious about experiencing a possible financial setback because it would likely force them to go without food to make ends meet, or quit school altogether.

This feeling of financial helplessness can easily continue into every stage of life.

GOING TO COLLEGE WAS NEVER SO COSTLY

To compound these issues, college costs have been increasing dramatically over the years. The average price of tuition, fees, and room & board for an undergraduate degree has gone up by 169% since 1980.

In 1980, attending a four-year college full-time cost only $10,231 a year, according to the National Center for Education[5]. This price includes tuition, fees, room and board.

Education, on average, was pretty affordable a short while ago, and students didn't have to bear a very high cost of living to maintain a certain standard. However, things have drastically changed over the decades, as today the yearly cost of attending college has increased to $28,775. It's almost tripled.

Additionally, the brand of education you choose will determine the prices you are subject to pay.

Universities charge more than other post-secondary institutions, and due to the lack of standardization in college prices, students who choose to study at private institutions (over public) have to pay even more to be a graduate.

According to data, the average cost of enrolling at a public university for the academic year of 2019-20 was $21,035, while it was $48,965 at a private nonprofit college.[5]

RISING STUDENT DEBT

The ever-inflating college costs have compelled students to owe exceedingly high amounts of student debt, which is now more than $1.5 trillion in the U.S. alone, second only to mortgage debt.[6]

We are only talking about the U.S.; this doesn't even include other countries.

On average, a person enrolled in college ends up with a student debt of more than $30,000—which is more than the credit card debt or auto loans that people usually have to pay off.

But this information does not only pertain to young people. There are older students who enroll in educational courses and acquire debt that sticks to them.

Surprisingly, students in the age bracket of 60–69 years old have been hit by a spike of 72% more student debt in the last decade.[7]

The numbers show that most college graduates will finish school already in debt, reaffirming the notion that enrolling in college can be a burden too heavy for most to bear.

But what are we to do?

Should you stop going to college to avoid taking out loans?

No.

Fortunately, you don't have to fear debt to the point of skipping college. If you want to get a college degree or want to pay for someone's college, you can manage your finances in a certain way to maintain financial peace of mind.

Let's explore the next step in a young student's financial journey — credit cards.

CREDIT CARDS COMPOUND THE CRISIS

The way you use credit cards can make a massive difference to your creditworthiness and long-term financial status.

Be aware that credit cards contribute significantly to the student loan crisis.

Banks make applying for credit cards a breeze of a task. It's so easy you often barely remember applying.

I recall one bright, sunny afternoon when I opened my first bank account on campus in college. It was my freshman year.

Up to this point in my life, I had never actually gone into a bank by myself. This was my first time!

I walked into the bank hoping to open one account.

That's it. No big deal. Just one account to put my money into.

I was expecting to get a checking account, and that's it.

By the time I left the bank, I had signed up for a checking account, savings account, brokerage account, and a credit card.

That's a total of four accounts! And I don't even remember how it happened.

It is pretty standard for young college students to own credit cards. It is almost second nature today. If you have a bank account, you likely have a credit card with the same bank.

Interestingly, 77% of colleges accept credit cards to pay for college tuition, which can present a host of financial issues if the collegiate doesn't understand how to manage their finances properly.[8]

Using a credit card to pay for college tuition may not be the best idea, as it may dupe unsuspecting students into paying off a lower-interest college loan with a high-interest credit card.

Therefore, it's important to realize this is one of the tactics banks use to squeeze money out of their young customers' pockets.

While most people do understand how to swipe a credit card, a significant number have no idea how to pay it back effectively.

Most do not realize how credit card interest works, and as a result, the banks make even more off their customers by adding interest each month the balance is due.

In 2020, it was reported that the average student owed $3,280 in credit card debt. Beyond that, 38% of them reported being behind on their payments. This type of debt was the source of most financial worries among students, even more so than student loans.[9]

This data indicates the lack of awareness and education about handling credit cards. And if we never learn how to use credit wisely, it's nearly impossible to avoid getting trapped in the perpetual cycle of "spend now, pay later" which can become a financial path of sinking sand that sucks you in for years.

DIRE NEED FOR FINANCIAL LITERACY

When we're younger and dependent on our parents for all of our needs, we have barely a clue about how money works in the real world.

It's only when we set off on our own, take up jobs, pay for school fees, and meet other day-to-day expenses that we get a sudden crash course on personal finance.

National Student Money found that 74% of students wished they had better financial education. The survey indicates that 65% of students who knew nothing about money management suffered from financial anxiety. Also, 76% of students considered dropping out of college due to mental health issues stemming from financial concerns.[10]

We aren't taught how to interact with high costs and limited resources as young kids.

As soon as you feel the urge to buy more than you can afford, the banks are right there at your service, making it incredibly easy to spend more money than you have in your bank account, and that's precisely where we falter.

As young adults, we get instant access to credit cards without an owner's manual or any required training. It's as though these companies are waiting for us to fail.

Going back to my earlier example—When I got my first (4) accounts at the bank, I happily took the credit card given to me without a second thought.

I didn't believe I needed any extra training. I was an A+ student in high school, and this 'money thing' seemed simple enough.

My basic knowledge told me, "When I use a credit card, pay the money back."

Enough said. I thought I had it all figured out.

But in my case, I never intended to use the credit card. And I never actually used the credit card while in college.

This particular credit card stayed tucked away in my drawer for all four years of college, and I used cash to pay for everything.

Once I finished college and started my journey after graduation, I soon squandered all my savings and started to use the credit card to make ends meet.

It never occurred to me to ask myself, "If I only choose to use a credit card when I need the money, how would I consistently pay the money back?"

That is a question I would not have been able to answer.

Since I "needed the money" each time I used the credit card, I also would "need the money" each time I earned income.

As I was so accustomed to using cash for my everyday expenses, paying off the credit card consistently seemed to be less of a priority. "As long as I make the minimum monthly payments, I can keep the credit card AND the cash." I thought to myself.

Of course, I was able to make the minimum payments each month on the credit card, but I realized (too late) that this was a losing strategy. My credit card balance was not going down, even though I was making payments. It seemed like my payments were not reducing the amount owed at all!

Within one year of graduation, this credit card was completely maxed out.

The card maxed out because I continued to use the credit card each month to make ends meet, even though I wasn't making enough income to consistently pay back the balance I had just utilized.

And boom... Just like that, I'm trapped by the first money villain— *mindless debt.*

This is precisely the story of millions of youngsters across the country.

As this story demonstrates, I graduated from my university financially illiterate.

There is a chance you would think I was a good student, since I passed all my classes in school and ultimately graduated. And maybe you would believe I was a decent teammate and society member, with me being an elected captain of the rugby team and president of a fraternity.

But I knew squat about money! I was a financial dufus.

Oddly enough, after college I decided to start a career as a financial agent. What irony!

Since I knew nothing about managing money for myself, I somehow assumed that becoming a part of the financial industry would be beneficial for me. This career path led me to another host of challenges, some of which I reveal in later chapters.

Believe it or not, it's quite common that your financial advisor may not be that great with money. They may also (like me when I got started) be financially illiterate. That's a story of another book, don't get me started on that!

This leads me to those we respect and love dearly, and hold in high regard. Let's focus on them for a moment... our parents and grandparents.

CREDIT CARD DEBT OUTPACES SAVINGS

So, what about our parents?

They are better off than their young adult children, right?

Not exactly.

Think about it like this: those who cannot develop financial prudence after they get out of high school and/or college will continue to live with a similar mindset over the years. Some adults lead a lifetime filled with problematic debt.

And since high schools and colleges rarely offer financial literacy courses, it's easy to see how adults would lack the resources to learn this information for themselves.

According to a study released in 2021, only half of Americans have more emergency savings than credit card debt. That means 1 out of every 2 people you know has more credit card debt than money saved.[11]

Also consider this, 73% of adults will continue to be in debt for life.[12]

Credit card debt can be a significant problem for anyone, regardless of age.

Whether it's our parents or so-called rich relatives, most households (upper-/middle-/lower-income) are more likely to have higher credit card debt than savings.

We live in an era where consumerism is highly celebrated and rewarded. We are conditioned to desire the nicest car, house, and clothes by any means necessary, even at the risk of being buried in debt.

If you fall into tough times and have a high-interest credit card to pay off, the debt spiral can get much worse.

When debt keeps piling up with no significant savings, it leads to worry and anxiety because you don't know what the future holds. If you have an emergency or an unforeseen event, you'll have no choice but to borrow money again and accumulate more debt.

This becomes an endless journey of credit card debt, and eventually subprime loans, which keep some folks terrified of facing their situation and correctly mapping and structuring a gameplan.

According to Experian, the average debt of more than 240 million Americans is $61,554, which gives a very gloomy picture of where we're headed.[12]

The fact that debt is an integral part of our finances goes to show it is almost pointless to try and avoid debt.

The real trick is learning to harness the system of money, and tip the scales in your favor.

BOOMERS' RETIREMENT DREAMS UP IN SMOKE

We've talked a little about our parents, but indeed our grandparents are safe, right?

Sorry to break it to you... here comes the bucket of cold water...

No one is safe. Not even your great-grandparents!

The money problems we've discussed thus far aren't only the reality for younger generations; even our baby boomers (our parents and grandparents) don't have the desired financial security.

Unfortunately, they're as clueless about how to win the money game as young adults are.

Remember, they come from a very different era, and likely still believe in the old mindset of relying only on academia and finding a "safe, secure" day job.

If we don't change how we think and act regarding personal finance, we'll remain stuck where we are—from generation to generation.

Quick question—If the baby boomers had this 'money thing' figured out, wouldn't they be living a life of ease and comfort by now?

Sadly, this is not the case for them.

According to a poll, baby boomers fear they may have to continue working all their lives and never retire. And at least one in four boomers have no plans to retire, ever.[13]

So much for safe, secure day job!

It now means safely working every day until you are securely buried in the dirt!

In fact, the majority of baby boomers have a greater fear of outliving their money than death. Yes, you read that right. Baby boomers would rather die than outlive their retirement savings.[14]

So when asked the question, "Which would you rather have happen to you? 1– Death, or 2– Living so long your savings deplete?" The answer that most baby boomers gave was "Death". Let that sink in.

Reportedly, 60% of people (age group 44 to 75) said they were insecure about their retirement. So realize that just because we grow older doesn't mean the world of financial abundance will magically unfold at our feet.

The idea of retiring (or being close to retirement) comes with several challenges all on its own: the markets are volatile, investments can be unstable, and situations like job loss and health issues can be unpredictable.

In addition, our living standards improve with each passing decade, and most retirees would like to maintain the same lifestyle, even after they cease to work full-time and are forced to live off their savings.

Retirees who have pensions to depend on will have an added sense of security than those who don't have pensions. But unfortunately, more and more workers face a retirement future that does not include employer pensions.[15]

If you need to build your own retirement fund, the journey can be quite challenging without proper financial planning.

IT'S TIME TO CHANGE

THIS IS YOUR WAKE-UP CALL TO DEVELOP YOUR KNOWLEDGE OF personal finance.

You may be advised to stick to the well-known ways of playing the money game, but if it hasn't entirely worked for the past generations, it's even less likely to work for you in our current economic times.

If you listen to the standard financial advice passed down by everyone else, you are likely to end up where everyone else is—working to pay off debt until you die.

Keep in mind that financial wisdom isn't something we are born with, nor is it hard to acquire. It's a skill developed by focused repetition, year after year, when no one is looking.

Develop this skill by continuing to remain curious and asking questions. Talk to experts (if you know anyone). Even if you can't find the information you are looking for, stay open to new insights by listening to great financial podcasts, reading finance blogs, and tuning into whoever teaches about personal finance.

For instance, if you'd like to learn how to get rid of your credit card debt, search for a video that talks about it in detail. Or suppose you want to learn from one person on every personal finance topic available. In that case, you may want to watch Marko's "WhiteBoard Finance" on YouTube and search for his most popular videos to jumpstart your development.

Remember, before making any significant financial decisions for your life, acquire a deep understanding to make the best choice.

Be easy on yourself. You are not going to get it perfect in the beginning. Developing new habits requires consistent attention and learning what it means to get it wrong.

Give yourself a chance to test new theories, try new ideas, and venture into the unknown. If you gather enough knowledge from the right resources, you will develop the confidence to manage your money in a way that fits exactly the person you are.

The combination of these ideas will place you squarely on the path to financial literacy.

When you are financially literate, you have total control over your finances. No matter how fast the cost of living rises or how many financial obligations you have on hand, you'll know what to do.

You will have the discipline to succeed. You'll realize you cannot have lasting financial freedom without financial discipline. You can choose the unique path that works for your life which leads you exactly where you are trying to go financially.[16]

By this point, you should have a great idea of how debt infiltrates our lives and follows us around. We can move on from this subject, thankfully!

But the cold water isn't quite finished yet...

There is a common belief that just making more money will solve all of your money issues.

Join me in the next chapter, where we reveal the truth behind the second "money demon" once and for all.

CHAPTER 2

WHAT IF I JUST MAKE MORE MONEY?

"A rich man is nothing but a poor man with money."

— W. C. FIELDS

There is a common belief that if you simply make more money, your financial life would be perfect. You would have more money to spend, more money to save, and more money to invest.

Makes perfect sense, right?

If you earned a higher income, you would be able to pay off any debt you have now, and then you would have a bunch of money left over that you could do anything with. In this dream life, you can live fully and die peacefully with cash to spare.

Why doesn't life automatically become like this for 100% of rich people?

Do you think celebrities play the money game better just because they earn millions of dollars each year?

Of course, making more money is a blessing, as it allows you to spend more freely. But this can be a problem too.

Every single person is at a disadvantage when they don't understand personal finance.

When you have too much money to spend but little financial wisdom, it's even easier to mismanage finances due to the magnitude of dollars involved.

An average person may consider an emergency something that will cost them $10,000 or less, whereas an emergency for a rich person may require $100,000 or more.

Another reason wealth without financial understanding is no good is because of the multitude that would love a big chunk of the wealth for themselves. Being rich may present more opportunities to give up your cash for a whole host of reasons (caused by the multitude).

There are iconic celebrities who you think would have no debts to pay, but turn out to be absolutely swamped in debt.

Michael Jackson, megastar of the music industry, died with over $400 million in debt. The fact that he sold 61 million albums in the U.S. couldn't prevent him from succumbing to the debt cycle.

Then there's 50 Cent, the rapper/actor, who had to file for bankruptcy in 2015, at the height of his career.

Also, oscar-winning actor Nicolas Cage was once worth $150 million but lost all of his money and eventually filed bankruptcy, owing the IRS $14 million in unpaid taxes.

It's hard to believe that people who create humongous wealth have no control over it. Sometimes it's the legal battles, other times it's extravagant purchases which cause them to lose money. Even crooks in their inner circle could secretly siphon money for years.[17]

Making more money doesn't guarantee financial literacy.

The cards are stacked against all of us when we don't know how to play the game of money. Hence, we need to understand the factors that plague high-income earners into losing at the game. Is it their outrageous spending habits? Is it poor financial planning?

Well, there can be multiple factors. But there's one area that needs your attention before it takes away all your wealth, especially if you are a high-income earner.

Allow me to introduce you to the second money villain— *taxes*.

HIGH INCOME EARNERS PAY UP IN TAXES

High-income earners are in extremely high tax brackets, which is why it's hard for them to escape the rat race. People who make $90,000 or above must pay at least 24% of their income to the Internal Revenue Service (IRS) in taxes, which is a whopping $21,600. The numbers get higher from there.[18]

If that was not shocking enough, you should know that people who earn over $540,000 per year owe the IRS almost 40% of their income, which is an astounding $216,000.

Imagine being a so-called "rich" person earning $540,000 during the year, and receiving a tax bill for $216,000! That's nearly half of your earnings.

All of a sudden: $540,000 in income doesn't go as far as you thought.

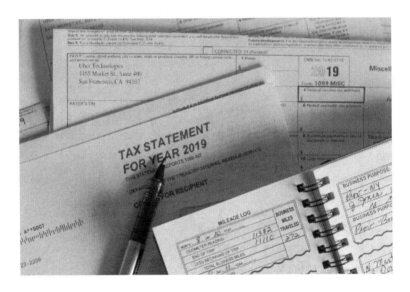

ATHLETES AND CELEBRITIES SLAMMED WITH TAXES

Reportedly, 78% of National Football League (NFL) players are in financial distress just two years after retirement, even though they've got the ability to reel in millions of dollars per year (and much more when including the endorsements deals).

After retirement, many athletes and celebrities go bankrupt, and their houses go into foreclosure.[19]

So, what's going on here?

Some of them have excessively lavish lifestyles and may spend money mindlessly. However, the insane amount of money they earn should ideally fund their fancies.

But taxes are a major issue for most professional athletes and celebrities, who usually have no financial education to help them understand taxes and find strategies to alleviate the burden.

THAT'S ONLY THE HALF OF IT

By the way, the earlier tax information is only referring to federal taxes.

Besides the federal taxes, professional athletes and celebrities lose even more money when paying state taxes. After state taxes are included, these high-income earners could easily pay taxes on more than 50% of their income.[20]

So, if somebody has to give away half of what they earn, no matter how much it is, they're bound to go broke unless they learn to live on half of their income from the very beginning.

Tax Revenue for State Governments

Athletes have the potential to make millions each day when they compete in a state other than their own, which is an excellent way for state governments to earn tax revenue.[21]

Most states in the U.S. aim to tax the maximum number of days the non-resident athletes are presumably on duty, which also typically includes travel days and any day after they arrive in the state.

This is in addition to paying the normal state taxes to the actual state where they live!

All athletes and entertainers need to pay separate state taxes for each state they visit and perform in, known as the "jock tax."

Pro athletes are required to file up to 25 tax returns every year.[22]

On average, an NFL player submits up to 12 non-resident state tax returns. A National Basketball Association (NBA) player files up to 20 such tax returns, while a Major League Baseball (MLB) player may file around 25.

Also, state tax revenue officials make it a focal point to target the athletes and celebrities who make the most money, since this tax brings in huge sums to the state.

Many times, there are unquestioned errors made by state tax revenue officials, and professional athletes and performers end up paying more in jock taxes than they're supposed to, due to a lack of financial knowledge.

SO MANY TAXES AND FEES, OH MY!

Even if we include all income earners, there are so many taxes you must be aware of.

Beginning with federal taxes, on average, an individual has to pay 17% of their total income as a federal tax. In addition, the average person pays about 10% of their income to state income taxes. Also, there are Medicare taxes to pay, which reduce their earnings by an additional 7.65%, and if you are self-employed, it's a 15.3% extra tax that you need to pay.[20]

After adding up all the taxes, you realize there's barely anything left in your paycheck.

The federal, state, and Medicare tax deductions extract 34.65% of the average employee's income. So, for instance, if somebody makes $60,000 annually, they get only $39,150 to spend after factoring in just these three tax deductions.

But it's not over yet. There's still more you're bound to pay in taxes.

If you're an employee and you decide to spend your "after-tax" income on something you need, get ready to pay more taxes!

You need to pay taxes on any vehicle you buy. If you choose to eat at a nice restaurant, the food you order is taxed. The coffee that you drink in the morning is taxed. The land you live on is taxed. The interest you earn from your "after-tax" investment in stocks is taxed too.

Here is a short list of the sort of taxes that an average American pays:

- Income tax
- Sales tax
- Bottle tax
- Bag tax
- Medicare tax
- Social security tax
- Gasoline tax
- Garbage tax

If this was not enough, there are all sorts of fees to pay, such as resort fees, driver's license fees, delivery fees, disposal fees, convenience fees, parking fees, HOA, and more.

There are over 97 taxes and fees we have imposed on our society.[23]

These taxes are complicated to understand for the average taxpaying American and even for tax professionals!

The modern tax system is designed so that, on average, out of every dollar earned, you will lose about 40 cents of that dollar to taxes before the dollar is even spent.

TAX RATES EXPECTED TO MOVE HIGHER

Many analysts believe tax rates are going up, so we can expect tax percentages to grow even more over time. From the 1950s to the 1970s, the highest tax rate for income was set at 70%. It was lowered to 39.6% in the 1990s. This means our current tax rates in the U.S. are at historical lows.[24]

The IRS modifies federal tax brackets according to the declining or rising cost of living. Since inflation surges with each passing year in the U.S. economy, the tax brackets are likely to be raised, too.

The maximum income tax rate was increased to 43.4% in 2012 due to the Affordable Care Act. The tax laws are constantly changing, and we could expect to see an increase in taxes throughout our lifetime.[24]

The real game changer in sparing your income from taxes will come once you acquire specialized knowledge on this subject.

You need to know how taxes work, what types of income are taxed, and learn about tax strategies to keep more than 60% of your income in the household during tax season.

You need to ask questions and get answers from the right sources. You may want to get in touch with an efficient and experienced accountant or a tax professional (perhaps someone who specializes in handling taxes for your industry or profession) who could educate and guide you.

Whether you work for a big company, own a business, work in the movies, or play football, making more money won't get you as far as you think after the IRS gets their share.

Taxes make a huge difference to your financial health. Thus, your tax strategy needs to be a crucial piece of your financial planning.

When you sit down to decide where you want to invest your money, consider taxes.

For instance, if your investments make profits and you sell them, you need to be aware of an additional capital gains tax.

Rich or poor, there is no way to avoid taxes altogether. Unless you decide to live in a cave and hunt mice.

However, there are intelligent ways to reduce your tax burden and retain more of your income. However, nothing is achievable without proper financial education and awareness.

High-income earners (and low-income earners) will easily fall into poor financial shape when the taxman comes to town if they do not have knowledge about tax saving strategies (which you will discover later in the book).

Nevertheless, bad debt and taxes are not the only two money villains we have.

There's a third money villain that works as an invisible threat we can't see.

Most of us cannot catch hold of this threat, and we lose the value of our money the longer we live.

Let's shine a light on this culprit in the next chapter.

CHAPTER 3

THE MOST SILENT OF ALL MONEY STEALERS

"Beware of little expenses. A small leak will sink a great ship."

— BENJAMIN FRANKLIN

L et's suppose you've covered all your bases up to this point. You earn a sufficient salary, you manage debt smartly, and you avoid taxes as much as possible. If you've experienced this much success in the money game, you are considered one of the fortunate ones. Some people may even call you lucky.

However, there is one final test that you have to take. And you'll have no study sessions, no answer key, and won't know whether you passed the test until years in the future.

This stealthy money demon never stops hovering around your nest egg, absorbing dollars year after year, right under your nose, through the rising prices of goods and services.

This money villain is known as *inflation*—and is the all-time greatest vulture of wealth.

If you never learn to defeat this third and final boss of the money villains, you will be fighting an uphill battle for life.

THE RISING COSTS OF GOODS

The costs of everything you can think of continues to get excessively expensive, so no matter how much we earn or try to reduce the debt burden, it seems we still don't have enough to buy the things we need.

The rapid pace at which inflation has risen recently has shocked many people. It's daunting to even attempt to plan a carefree retirement life because we are no longer sure exactly how much savings will be required.

The traditional notion tells you to save a percentage of your income every month, after taxes, to help prepare you for retirement. That notion makes a lot of common sense, until you factor in inflation.

With inflation, we no longer know how much our money will be worth in the next ten years. Will prices continue to increase exponentially over that timespan? Will the prices of goods and services ever stagnate and give our savings a chance to catch up?

Nevertheless, savings alone can no longer carry the load of your retirement goals and financial independence. The inflation storm lurking behind the previous two money villains is strong enough to cripple the most diligent saver's money pot.

This chapter will especially help those who believe you can simply save your way through the storm known as inflation.

But first, we need to address those who are not currently saving money consistently.

Let's break this down, because even though inflation kills the value of our money, there are still many great reasons why you should primarily focus on developing a habit of saving money.

Saving money is a great area to focus on if you have not already developed this habit, since this one skill will propel you ahead financially in a dramatic fashion.

Studies show that 78% of workers live paycheck to paycheck, while one in four workers don't set aside any savings at all.[25]

If you haven't learned how to regularly set aside money for emergencies and future goals, you are still at the mercy of the first two money villains.

You won't even be able to reach this level to face the third money villain yet, until you've developed enough financial discipline to conquer the villains mentioned previously.

But unfortunately, this doesn't mean you can ignore inflation.

On the contrary, inflation confronts everyone whether you are saving or not.

The prices of goods and services will not wait for you to get it together before they start rising higher, increasing the difficulty level of the money game.

With finances being the #1 cause of mental health issues[26], one solid remedy to decrease money stress and anxiety from your mind is to develop a savings habit and build an emergency fund.

Set aside 3 to 6 months' worth of household expenses (up to one year's worth) into a separate savings account.

The earlier you start, the more time you'll have to accumulate a large amount of money over time. You need to contribute a reasonable (consistent) amount every month.

THE 50/30/20 RULE

So, how much should you save to be on the right track?

While saving can be subjective for each individual according to their unique situation, there's a budgeting technique, or a saving method, to help you get started.

It's called the 50/30/20 rule, which recommends spending 50% of your total monthly income (net income, after taxes) on your necessary expenses, 30% on your wants/desires, and save the remaining 20% for savings and any debt payment.[27]

According to the 50/30/20 rule, if your monthly take-home pay is $5,000, you should use $2,500 for your fixed expenses, spend $1,500 on fun things, and set aside $1,000 for savings and/or debt repayment.

But this rule is not a one-size-fits-all. For some of you, you will need to start with less than 20% savings per month, for others you should start with more.

It's more important that you develop the habit of saving and being disciplined with your money.

As an aside, you shouldn't focus on saving money at the cost of not eating well and neglecting your health. You can live frugally without compromising your quality of life.

There is a general misconception that living frugally means not spending any money at all. But that's not true. Living frugally means making the best use of the resources available to you and making the most of every dollar you have.

To learn over 20 methods to save money with things you do every day, visit www.101MoneySecrets.com to get your free copy of 101 Money Secrets.

SAVINGS MISCONCEPTIONS

When discussing this idea of savings, you have to get the message that saving money will only get you so far.

You should save money to develop financial discipline. But you should also understand that it is a myth that you can just save your way to an early retirement, and live a baller lifestyle in your golden years.

And this is a myth that you will hear from family, friends, teachers, and colleagues.

For example, Fidelity, a large investment company, has a guideline for retirement savings, which suggests that your retirement fund should have at least six times your annual salary by age 50; and by age 67, your retirement fund should have ten times your annual salary.[28]

Unfortunately, this outdated way of thinking about personal finance has a couple of flaws.

Firstly, one simple question is: How do you calculate a person's annual salary in these times?

It seems you must base an annual salary on what a person is earning today; however, in the next 10, 20, or 30 years that salary number has to be much higher. But how much higher? This is where inflation trips us up.

However, continuing with Fidelity's guidelines, let's assume you stop working at age 67 and have accumulated ten times your annual salary.

What happens after year 10?

If you live off your savings for the entire ten years, what happens for the next ten years?

Do you start working part-time at age 78?

Maybe now we can understand why most retirees can honestly admit they would rather die than live long enough to face this situation.

Another savings misconception is that when you're trying to get ahead financially, you should "save even more", and that will solve all your money woes.

BEING A "SUPER SAVER"

Some people take it to an extreme level by saving everything they can. These ambitious "super savers" manage to save 50% or more of their monthly income each month.[29]

While saving half of your earnings every month may be an idea to get rid of debt faster and retire earlier, it's only recommended for those who can live comfortably on only 50% or less of their income. This is a small minority of people.

Keep in mind that there's no right or wrong way to save. Everybody has their comfort zones when it comes to saving, and it's perfectly okay to be able to save only a small percentage. The most important thing is you must develop the habit.

Thus, you shouldn't feel discouraged because you've got a few liabilities and expenses to take care of before you can begin saving a more significant percentage of your income. Just start with a modest amount, and build your way up.

Each individual should consider their own life, resources, support system, and household income before committing to any extreme saving style.

Now there are two sides of the coin when it comes to the topic of saving.

One side of the coin says, "Saving money is a habit that is very important which you need to develop", while the second side of the coin reads, "Saving money alone is not going to secure your financial freedom".

We will dig into both sides to help you understand the dynamic at play.

You need to have a complete picture of what saving means from a positive and negative perspective before you are able to truly combat this third money villain known as inflation.

MANY GREAT REASONS TO SAVE MONEY

Saving money is an essential habit that you need to develop. Here's why you should start saving at least some amount regularly:

- Once you start saving money consistently, you will begin to see how quickly you can accumulate money.
- Saving will give you confidence in your ability to manage money. The larger your savings account grows, the more your mentality will expand.

- When you accomplish your saving goals, it gives you a sense of achievement, which builds your self-confidence and promotes good mental well-being.[30]
- When you're disciplined about saving, it helps you stay up-to-date with paying all your bills on time, managing debt sensibly, and setting financial goals to pay for your future desires.
- The more you save money, the more mindful you will become about spending on things that will reduce your savings. You will avoid making purchases driven by peer pressure.
- You can teach good money habits to the youth who haven't yet begun earning their own income yet. When the proper saving habits are passed on to somebody still young, they can incorporate it into their life much more seamlessly.

Think of the savings habit as a stepping stone to your financial freedom. Saving money is not a burden, but it's also not the "end-all-be-all". It's just one aspect of your healthy financial decisions.

There's more that you need to do; however, the foundation of your financial health has to be saving.

SAVING MONEY IS NOT ENOUGH

While saving is the foundation of creating wealth, it's not enough. You must realize that you cannot "save your way" to financial freedom.

This next part may come as a shock, but it's the cold water truth.

According to a study conducted by Bank of America, one in four millennials have at least $100k saved, but 73% of those surveyed said they still felt that they lagged far behind their peers in terms of securing their financial future.[31]

So even though people are making financial progress by building great savings habits and large emergency funds, they still feel insecure about their financial future.

What's up with that?

This is where inflation kicks into high gear.

You cannot depend on savings alone because:

- The considerable risk of saving in traditional retirement plans, such as the 401(k), is that they are exposed to market risk, and we have seen our close acquaintances and relatives lose large portions of their retirement value due to recessions and the latest pandemic.[32]
- If you simply leave your money in bank accounts, your money will lose value due to inflation. The interest rates (usually around 0.01%) that a savings account pays on your money is much lower than the growing inflation rate (over 7%).
- Stocks and mutual funds are subject to volatile swings in the economy which cause our account balances to go up and down. These accounts may or may not lose against inflation; it's a gamble. The account must continue to go up over the long run to keep pace with inflation.

- By leaving your money to stay in one place for long periods of time, you're missing out on opportunities to multiply it exponentially.

WHEN INFLATION COMES TO TOWN

Here's the scenario that brings about inflation: First, the cost of production increases, and the prices of goods and services go up. Secondly, the currency we hold is not able to buy as many goods and services (our purchasing power declines), so the currency we hold is worth less than before.

Two phenomena related to inflation impact the economy, and eventually our spending. The first phenomenon of inflation is the rising cost of living, while the second is the declining purchasing power.

Let's pull back the curtain on these inflation factors, starting with the rising cost of living, and how the price of necessities increase faster than our earnings, which lag behind.

Let's rewind a couple decades and go back to the year 2000, when the average cost of a gallon of gas was $1.52.[33]

Fast forward to 2022, only 22 short years later, and we see gas prices have increased by 330%. Currently, gas prices have topped $5 per gallon and have continued to rise.[34]

The cost of living increases faster than median wages, meaning people from all income groups bear the impact of rising prices to some extent.

In the last two decades, gas prices have increased by 330%, while median household incomes have only increased by 40%. Besides, there are many other expenses that have continued to grow over the years, such as groceries, real estate, dining out, plane tickets, and a host of other items.[35]

When inflation occurs, virtually all prices of consumer goods go up[36]. Therefore, the money you put into your savings account today will lose its value with each passing day.

Inflation is especially alarming for those who rely solely on their savings accounts and have fixed incomes. We witnessed a drastic 8.2% rise in the cost of consumer goods in the fiscal year of April 2021 to April 2022. This indicates the highest rate of inflation in the last 40 years.

However, when it comes to average wages, the increase was only a minor boost of 4.5% in that year. So, wages actually declined by 1.5% when adjusting for inflation.[37]

Hence, your ability to buy goods decreases with time due to the acceleration of rising costs. If you had a large amount of money saved ten years ago, that cash could have afforded you more goods and services (back then) than that same amount of money will afford you today.

This leads us to the second factor of inflation, which is the declining purchasing power.

IMPACT OF PURCHASING POWER

Purchasing power determines your ability to buy goods and services with the amount of money you have available. When inflation hits, prices go up, and the money you have isn't able to purchase as much as it could have before inflation hit.[38]

Typically, a currency's purchasing power declines due to inflation and increases due to deflation (a decrease in the prices of goods and services). You can pray for deflation, but it seems that we are accustomed to inflation, and must learn to accept it.

To understand how purchasing power works, think of a scenario where you are earning the same income 20 years from now that you are making today. Your income does not increase a single cent in 20 years.

What do you think life would be like?

One thing is for sure; you wouldn't be able to afford the same amount of goods and services that you can afford today.

Now, why is that? It's because of the weakening purchasing power over the decades.

For example, the first 8GB iPhone was released in 2007 for a price of $499. Today, the brand new 128GB iPhone 14 Pro starts at $999.

There are many more bells and whistles on the latest smartphones today. However, the first iPhone in 2007 was the latest and greatest invention of its time, and the smartphones that will be released 20 years from now will also have many more bells and whistles that we can't imagine today.

One thing we can predict, however, is that the price tag will be higher. The price tag will likely double again in the next couple decades.

As prices increase, the pile of money saved in the mattress, or sitting in a bank account, loses its purchasing power (by a lot). If you aren't prepared for this, the rising costs will affect your standard of living and add more stress to your financial health.

THE RULE OF 72

A simple way to understand how interest rates impact the value of money is through the Rule of 72. This is a formula you can use to determine the years it will take for your money to double at a specific interest rate.[39]

The idea is to apply the formula to anything that provides an interest rate of return on your money. Using the Rule of 72, you can also figure out how fast your money will lose its value based on the current inflation rate.

All you need to do to calculate this formula is divide the number 72 by an expected rate of return to get a rough idea of the duration of time it takes your money to double:

Suppose you've invested $1,000 with an expected interest rate of 12%.

72 ÷ 12 = 6 years

So your $1000 will grow to $2,000 in six years (assuming you receive 12% compounding growth each year).

And if you keep your $2000 growing here, and it continues to double every six years (at the consistent interest rate of 12%), then it will grow to $4,000 in 12 years, $8,000 in 18 years, and so on.

Also realize, the lower your expected rate of return is, the longer it will take to double.

So for a more realistic example, let's see how long it will take money to grow in the average savings account offering 0.01% interest.

$72 \div .01 = 7200$ years

Ouch!

7200 years though?!

You would probably have to die and come back to life 368 times before that $1000 would grow into $2000.

And by the time your money doubled once in the savings account (7200 years in the future), $1000 would likely be worth closer to what a penny is worth today, because of inflation.

You could imagine people walking over $1000 in the street, 7200 years in the future. It wouldn't even be worth the time (and embarrassment) to bend over and pick up $1000 off the ground.

Because of this, you might understand why many people hate the big banks.

Banks give you as small of a rate of return on your money as possible (0.01%), and turn around and offer your money right back to you (in the form of credit and loans) for interest rates up to 20% or higher.

. . .

INFLATION AND THE RULE OF 72

When I started learning about personal finance, the rule of 72 was the first concept I was taught. It's a great way to gauge the trajectory of my savings growth and make smarter financial decisions.

Over time, I realized that when most people talk about the rule of 72, they only discuss how it can help your portfolio grow over the years. This formula is usually explained in terms of "how long it takes your money to double".[40]

This is an easy way to grasp the concept of this formula.

However, the rule of 72 can also be applied to how inflation impacts your money—it shows you how fast your money can decrease in value over a period of time based on the increasing rate of inflation.

So for example, in March 2022, the annual inflation rate jumped to 8.5%.[41]

So, if we use the rule of 72 on that rate of inflation (which is 72 ÷ 8.5 = 8.47), we see that our money will lose half of its value every 8-9 years!

So apparently, the old adage is wrong—a penny saved is NOT a penny earned.[42]

A penny saved is only worth about half a penny in the next ten years.

If we return to the typical inflation rates of ~4%, a dollar you save today will lose half of its value in 20 years, and will only be worth about $0.44 in the next two decades.

But if we consider the current state of affairs, 8% inflation will reduce $1 to $0.44 in just ten years!

Don't forget, this money villain is happening right now as you read these words, in addition to the two money villains mentioned earlier. If you're getting beaten by taxes and beaten by debt, how do you expect to beat inflation?

This third money villain is on another level. But there are simple steps you can take to control this beast, and put yourself ahead of it each year.

NOW YOU ARE READY FOR MORE

If you've stayed with me up to this point, and I haven't scared you off, round of applause to you. You are ready to separate yourself from the average money gamers out there.

You now know the financial ailments that plague us all, and you are ready for the medicine!

Yes, you are reading the right book.

Don't worry, there is light at the end of the tunnel.

You have to understand what the financial darkness looks like and how most people end up there, before you can interpret the light, and discover the unique path to bring yourself to it.

Become Familiar With The Fundamentals

As stated earlier, it's important to know the playing field you're on before you can make any intelligent moves to get anywhere better. Awareness and confidence are essential to overcome challenges and put yourself in a position to win.[43]

Since you are familiar with the pitfalls in the personal finance world, you can decide to choose a path different from how the majority of people are doing things. You will have the awareness to know how to avoid pitfalls early on, before it's too late.

Some of the beginning information may have sounded pretty basic for some of you. Nevertheless, it's incredibly important that you do not ignore the basics.

If you ignore the basics, you'll not have the diligence and precision to conquer the money villains. It will become easier for you to lose the vision of why you're making certain money moves. This makes it more likely to experience financial missteps and waste your time.

Knowing the basics helps you stay vigilant with your decisions and take calculated risks. Even if you make mistakes, your determined mentality allows you to learn from them and emerge stronger.

Before we proceed further, here's a heads up: This book is not meant to teach you the exact path to "getting rich" or a step-by-step of how to choose the exact products and investments that are right for you. The closest thing you will find, as far as tangible actions you can implement for yourself, will be found at: www.101MoneySecrets.com

FYI: Some of those secrets are advanced processes, which will not be helpful to those who don't understand the fundamentals of money, first and foremost.

To Become A Master, Master The Basics

Subjects such as "Getting rich fast" or "Investing in products or businesses" are advanced lessons that may cause more harm than good, without first having a solid foundation of financial knowledge.[44]

In fact, don't even think about attempting advanced processes until you learn the basics.

This is similar to asking Phil Jackson (Hall of Fame coach) to teach you how to play an organized game of team basketball for the very first time in your life, and you show up demanding your very first lessons to be about how to make half-court jump shots.[45]

No, bro.

It would be best if you learned the basics first, like how to dribble, how to perform a bounce pass, how to catch a ball with good form, how to use proper footwork to transition into a layup, etc.

You mustn't start your journey into basketball by mindlessly hoisting hail-mary shots at the basket (which is what many new investors do in the personal finance realm).

I see many new investors (even myself at the beginning), who jump into investment vehicles without proper education and get crushed simply because of their lack of knowledge.

They make investment choices based on somebody else's gains or just because something seems to be trending. They forget the fact that any investment requires a thorough understanding to fully maximize the benefits and counteract the negatives.

The cardinal rule of investing is to stay away from investing in something you don't understand—and since you may not fully understand how money works, you aren't yet ready to begin an intelligent approach to investing in anything.[46]

Furthermore, if you don't have a 1000% understanding of how an investment will help you overcome the three money villains, then you are gambling.

Speaking of gambling, in the next chapter you will learn how common it is for the general population to be unknowingly forced into gambling when it comes to personal finance.

Also, we will go inside the mind of successful gamblers to explain how they are able to tip the casino's edge in their favor.

It's getting interesting...

You don't want to miss this!

CHAPTER 4
THE CASINO'S ADVANTAGE

"Money won't create success, the freedom to make it will."

— NELSON MANDELA

B efore you learn how to become rich or how to retire early, you need to understand that there are quite a few money stealers, which we have shed light upon in the last three chapters.

Mindless debt, taxes, and inflation are the top three financial pitfalls that the majority of people fall victim to. Hence, they're never able to rise above them to savor financial independence.

The secret to winning the game of money is knowing the obstacles that make you stumble and learn to confront them head-on. Defeat these three money villains, and you will succeed in the game of money. Let's quickly recap these villains.

Debt is something that many young students get accustomed to as soon as they enter college, and a negative mentality is developed toward debt. However, a certain amount of debt isn't destructive or harmful if you know how to handle it.

Debt is bad only when you pay high interest on the amount you owe, and it goes on for a long time. If you can quickly pay off your debt at a low interest rate, it doesn't become a burden.

Unfortunately, most people cannot manage debt prudently because they lack financial awareness and knowledge.

Using multiple credit cards and allowing interest to accrue on each balance is a bad practice that we can get addicted to quite early on, costing us our mental health and the power to plan a financially stable life.

 Taxes take away such a massive chunk of our income (especially for high-income earners) and can cause us to feel stuck in our careers with no escape. Athletes, especially, end up paying all sorts of taxes because they aren't aware of the tax-saving tactics.

If any person is forced to give away almost 40% of their income toward taxes, there's very little left to take care of expenses, debt repayment, savings, and investments.

Inflation keeps you running on a treadmill (in the same spot) because it reduces your purchasing power over the years. When things get expensive, and you still need to buy them, you spend much more than you're capable of.

Additionally, the growth rate of your savings is not as fast as the soaring prices of all sorts of goods and services.

NO ONE IS SAFE FROM THE VILLAINS

It's easy for anyone to fall victim to one, if not all, of these money villains. Even financially licensed professionals can unknowingly succumb to the pitfalls. There are financial advisors from Charles Schwab who have admitted to making bad financial decisions and filing for bankruptcy.[47]

Financial planners can also get tripped up by the money villains, including owing excessive debt and attracting large tax bills. However, this is not to say they aren't qualified to advise you on handling your finances and what to avoid.

Remember, no matter who you're consulting, apply your innate wisdom and understanding to make your decisions.

Even So-Called Professionals Fail

The Certified Financial Planner (CFP) Board takes it a step further and keeps a list of all licensed financial planners who have filed for bankruptcy at some point. You will find new names added to this list each year.[48]

It may come as a surprise that many licensed agents in the money profession have failed in their own personal finances. Everybody is capable of making mistakes. Nobody is perfect. A financial pitfall, like bankruptcy, may happen to any person for a number of reasons. It isn't necessarily indicative of a financial professional's character or trustworthiness.

Even within my financial agency, I knew higher-ups in banks and some of the largest financial firms. I led a team with over 50 agents and visited hundreds of clients' homes, delivering financial tips.

At the time, I thought I had finally figured out the money game, but I still eventually found myself buried in debt and forced to file bankruptcy after hitting rock bottom.

Although it's commonly believed that personal bankruptcy is a thing of the poor and middle-class folks, it's very much the reality for the upper middle class and high net worth individuals.[49]

Personal bankruptcies might not be discussed regularly, but they exist in great numbers. Reportedly, America has seen a surge in bankruptcies since 2006, as the number of non-business bankruptcy filers totaled almost 400,000 in 2021.[50]

WE LOSE BECAUSE WE GAMBLE

Why are so many people (including those who are supposed to know about money the most) still stumbling into financial pitfalls?

It's because most of us are taught to play the money game as though we were gambling, leading us to place risky bets just like we do in a big casino.

Many gamblers are unaware that casinos have every single game calculated into mathematical odds, which are all against the player.

The casino makes most of its income through the losses of players. So, casino games are deliberately designed to give the player a losing edge. The house has the advantage.

A house's advantage may vary from game to game, and a player can win from time to time; however, over the course of days, weeks, and months, the casino has the statistical advantage. The longer you play the game, the more likely you are to lose all the money you bet.[51]

A gambler should know that the casino is always prepared to win because of the math already computed into their games. Casinos know that the players will lose most of the rounds, and have calculated the amount of money per hour that the average player should lose. Not just this, but they also know that the amount of money you're going to win will be lower than the amount you will lose over time.

Similarly, the money game of life is set up with the odds stacked against us. It's a game we're designed to lose. Most people lose the money game because they treat it like a risk-free gamble.

They buy stocks without knowledge and research, they make investments they don't believe in, or they never invest due to fear of the markets, they use credit cards without caution, they procrastinate saving for the future, etc. There are plenty of ways to lose the money game.

When you operate without understanding and wisdom, you win only by luck; however, you're more likely to lose. On the other hand, if you're vigilant about how the economy functions and stay abreast of its loopholes, you can overcome any hurdle and make the most of every penny you earn.

ADVANTAGE GAMBLING

Once you know the playing field and learn how to tip the odds in your favor, you can play the money game on an evolved level. In the casino world, this is referred to as "advantage gambling."

The casino gives all players the same odds to win, even though they're not very good odds. So everyone is on the same plane to start. Next, it's up to the player to understand the tricks and legal loopholes, and use them to their advantage.

So, what's an example of this in the casino world?

Firstly, when you study how to play certain casino games, there are techniques for playing the game to minimize the house's edge.

Secondly, a player can use the comps and rebates that a casino offers to its 'players club' members to tip odds in their favor and give themselves a slightly increased betting advantage over the casino.[52]

Therefore, if players are able to play the casino game(s) in a disciplined manner to minimize the house's edge, with the combination of the comps and rebates, there's a possibility of getting a minimal edge over the casino.

Third, you can increase your odds even more by playing during promotional periods offered by casinos. There are opportunities for a player to earn double points for a round. This allows the player to boost the slight edge that they've already got.

Furthermore, the casino has a game called Blackjack, which has a smaller house edge than the rest of the casino games. If you learned how to flip the casino's edge in your favor, you could win consistently if you played the game of blackjack in a certain way.

There are professional blackjack players who earn upwards of $180,000 per year, simply by playing this game with a specific technique, which is entirely different from the way that the majority of people play blackjack.[53]

So, it's all about learning the proper techniques and applying them consciously. Those who 'gamble' in the gambling world lose their money most of the time. However, those who 'gamble' with a particular methodology can maximize their wins and even make a good living.

FIND YOUR EDGE IN THE MONEY GAME

Similar to playing casino games in a way that is different from the majority, you can successfully play the money game of life in a certain way and give yourself an advantage over the house.

You've got everything working against you—especially debt, taxes, and inflation—so if there's any chance you can find an advantage, it would be wise to implement it for yourself.

If you manage your finances just like everybody else, you're not going to achieve anything different.

Remember that it's okay to make mistakes and lose sometimes.

Even professional casino players still suffer losses. Just because they are professionals, and play the casino for a living, doesn't mean they win every bet.

The professionals understand that it's a long game. All it takes is discipline, confidence, and consistency. But there needs to be a realization that even Hall of Famers suffer temporary losses. Be open to learning from failure.

Use losses as an opportunity to sharpen your skills. Ask more questions, absorb more information, revisit your goal(s), and return wiser and sharper.

Now, before we learn about the financial strategies you can implement to defeat the money villains, we have to talk about the financial industry, as there will be financial companies you will (eventually, if not already) be using for certain products.

There's something fundamental about the financial industry that's rarely spoken about, which will help you understand why I eventually walked away from the industry at the height of my career.

Let's find out all about it in the next chapter.

CHAPTER 5
"YOUR PRODUCT SUCKS" SAYS THE AGENT

"Money is only a tool. It will take you wherever you wish, but it will not replace you as the driver."

— AYN RAND

There's raging competition taking place in the financial industry today.

Financial companies and professionals are fiercely contesting to see who can get the most clients and make the most sales.

This competition can lead agents to make tall claims to their clients. They will promise higher than average rates of returns, no-fee deals, or investment products with no hidden charges.[54]

In this wild west of finance, sometimes the only thing the professional cares about is selling a product and securing their commission.

Usually, a financial agent will give specific product recommendations based on one of three factors:

1. Company Limitations (that's all their company offers);
2. Familiarity (that's the product(s) they like the most); or
3. Payouts (that's the product(s) with the most generous commissions)

This goes for whether you're working with bankers, brokers, or other financial professionals.

Realize you may not get a product recommendation that fits perfectly with your personal finance strategy. And it's important to know that most financial agents are trained salesmen. It's all about making the best pitch and closing the sale.

If you go to somebody to get the best possible financial advice to make your money grow, make sure they educate you, first and foremost, before you consent to get started with any product.

You must understand that the financial industry doesn't agree on which financial strategy is best. One company will tell you Product X is the best in the industry, while another will say to you Product Z is the best in the industry.

It's your responsibility to be aware of their selling tactics and protect your cash from being tied up in financial instruments until you are 100% certain that it fits with your overall financial strategy.

While there's no harm in seeking an expert's opinion on how to invest and plan for a better financial future, you should also do your own research.

Everyone's situation is unique in terms of their background, the amount of money they make, the kind of value system they have, and the sort of goals they have in mind. Thus, you can have a financial product that gives different results for different people.

One person could have enormous success with a financial product, while another person does not have any success, and must try something else. You need to figure out what's currently available and make conscious decisions to talk to the right people.

To make the right decision of choosing the right insurance or investment instrument, you need to be aware that the agent sitting opposite you isn't usually interested in what's absolutely best for you. Instead, they have the incentive to make money by selling you something. Hence, you need to make your own choices and not fall for products you didn't intend to buy, and haven't had the chance to research.

GOOD COMMUNICATION VS. FINANCIAL LITERACY

According to the CPA Journal, the leading quality inherent in top-ranked financial planners is the ability to build relationships and communicate in a friendly, persuasive way in order to sell to clients more effectively.[55]

Notice that the number one skill is not about being a good teacher, understanding the products being sold, or being financially savvy.

The best financial planners are known to communicate in a manner that helps them sell more products. However, this skill does not mean they're good with money matters or have a thorough understanding of the products they sell.

So if you happen to interact with a financial agent who makes an excellent sales pitch to you (that makes you want to buy the product immediately), remind yourself to take a step back to breathe, and make sure you can do enough research to make a confident decision.

How Is This Important?

Some of you may think this subject is irrelevant at this stage of the journey, since you don't intend to be in these sorts of encounters. So let's address that idea.

If you have made it this far into the book AND you have never been in a situation where someone is trying to sell you on taking action on a business decision immediately... CONGRATULATIONS!

You should consider yourself one of the luckiest people alive.

It's quite common to find yourself in this situation as you grow older. And it can happen when you least expect it.

For myself, I was sold on my first financial products when I was 18 years old (at the bank in college). I was sold on my first business investment when I was age 19.

What I wish I had known back then, and trying to help you discover now, is that most businessmen and businesswomen do not have the money game figured out. The competition to most of them is about getting more sales, more recruits, and more clients.[56]

This is not to say don't trust anyone who presents you with a financial opportunity. This is to say proceed with caution, and maintain financial discipline. Two things I did not follow in those earlier years. But you don't have to make the same mistakes.

Nonetheless, it would be best if you desired to know how to handle your own money before seeking any professional advice.

Let's bring our attention to how this affects the typical customer in the financial industry.

FINANCIAL LITERACY IS NOT THE PRIORITY

Since there's fierce competition amongst financial companies in the marketplace, numerous financial products have emerged for people to pick from.

However, most financial companies care more about simply selling products than teaching financial literacy. When customers don't know what's right for them, they can't make informed decisions. Most clients accept whatever is sold to them without realizing what they've bought.

Financial agents try their best to make money through their clients because that's their best source of recurring revenue. Ambitious financial professionals persuade their clients on products, while the clients blindly follow the lead of the professional without fully understanding how to take advantage of the product.

Realize that companies within the financial industry are not paid to teach financial literacy. They are paid to make sales and generate revenue.

This is especially true for large financial organizations that have a ticker symbol and trade on a stock exchange. If their company has a stock, this company works for their shareholders. And what do shareholders want? More money, more profits, more revenue, and increased stock prices—which increase the net worth of the shareholders.

As a side note: The competition in the financial industry can help the efficiency and enhancement of products you are offered[57]. So there is definitely a gain for clients as the financial products have improved over the years.

However, if the clients are still lacking in their knowledge of how to maximize the benefits and lower the downsides of the products they own, the enhanced products will sit on the shelf to collect dust in the lives of the clients.

Once again, this boils down to the core of financial growth— which is financial literacy—it's your sole weapon against the economic situations you will face.

Be careful of banks and other financial institutions that try to sell products that don't make sense to you. You should also be aware that bank employees are trained to use pressure tactics to get customers to apply for products they don't need or understand.

For evidence, research the class action lawsuits which discovered Wells Fargo and Bank of America were found to sell products and open accounts in customers' names without their consent.[58]

FairShake conducted a recent study which shows that at least 16 different banks are hated in each U.S. state for various reasons, such as bad customer service, false promises, misleading information, hidden fees, unexplained charges, and long holds on deposits.[59]

Even though there are many financial institutions to choose from, most customers have had negative experiences dealing with all of them, regardless of which one you choose.

Does this mean every financial institution is "out to get you"?

Of course not.

Many people who work for these companies are well-meaning, kind-hearted individuals.

Just remember, simply because they are working in the industry does not make them financially literate. They could easily be financially illiterate with excellent persuasive skills. And if you put your financial lives in their hands without being completely aware of what you are getting into, you could be left bearing the brunt of their financial miscues.

Remember, financial professionals are under steady pressure to continually sell products. It's up to you to understand how/when to take advantage of what's being offered.

TWO DIFFERENT LANGUAGES, TWO DIFFERENT GOALS

For the average young adult seeking financial advice, studies show the most common topics of discussion include:

- When can I stop working, or retire sooner?
- How do I develop an investment strategy?
- How do I use retirement money effectively?
- How do I budget for retirement expenses?
- What type of insurance do I need, and how much?

Realize that most of these topics are about how to retire. These questions are not solely focused on products. Customers want clarity on how to navigate the money villains.

Therefore, you can understand why this study also reported that young adults feel "more confused than ever" due to the "wide range of offerings" in the marketplace.

It's two different languages being spoken between the two parties—clients and professionals—and two different goals between the two parties.

Clients desire financial professionals to teach them how to be financially literate, while financial professionals are trained to look for every opportunity to recommend products.

Unfortunately, customers aren't advised on their genuine concerns. They're told to buy products, which makes their financial situation no better.[60]

Getting into more investment products without the proper education doesn't ingrain any lasting confidence in customers because most of the time they don't remember what they've gotten into or how it fits into their overall financial gameplan.

One Of My Most Memorable Appointments

In my tenure as a financial agent, I would have sales meetings with clients, where I would figure out what products they currently had, and tell them what product they should buy next, or why a particular product was better than what other companies were offering.

Here is a fascinating story of something that happened to me on one of these sales visits...

So I went to meet with a customer at Starbucks. He had questions about what he should do for retirement, and I had recommendations that I wanted to show him.

Just as our meeting started, another financial agent walked by our table, noticed the customer, and came over to start a conversation. I don't know if this was a coincidence because the other financial agent just happened to be from a competing company.

The competing agent and the customer started casually talking, catching up on old times, until the conversation switched to the subject at hand, the reason for our meeting.

Instantly, the competitor agent had a story to tell about how he just had a client the other day who was dissatisfied with one of my company's products, and switched to his company because his products were cheaper and had no hidden fees.

What the competitor agent didn't know was that I had witnessed the exact opposite. I had current clients who decided to switch from his competing company and work with me because my products were cheaper and more suitable.

I didn't realize at the time how normal this dynamic is in the financial industry.

For example, most licensed professionals in the financial industry will only recommend the products that their company is selling. A financial planner will have a particular set of products they believe to be the best, and insult a financial advisor based on the advisor's product recommendations, even if the planner has never worked as a financial advisor. And vice versa.

However, in the meeting at Starbucks, I wasn't ready for this surprise attack.

I didn't know if what the competing agent was saying was true, but this was an inopportune time for me to debate with him. Unfortunately, this is the industry culture. Present your arguments, or lose clients.

The other agent was a better communicator than me in this situation—prepared to attack me with dubious claims about my product recommendations while stating that theirs were superior.

For a while, the other agent and I started arguing about who was better, and that went on for the entire meeting I had at Starbucks that day. The poor client left the meeting more confused than before he showed up.

My tenure as a financial agent taught me the cold, hard truth that we are all trained in the industry to persuade and sell clients into products. We are essentially salesmen and saleswomen with certifications and licenses. Glorified marketeers.

Fortunately, financial products have infinitely improved over the years, for reasons stated earlier. So it's still a great idea to know someone in the industry.

But the realization of my own motivations, and how I was being groomed into focusing on my sales numbers and agency growth, forced me to ponder the core problems in the financial landscape and think about more comprehensive financial literacy solutions that I could offer.

Another pattern I noticed in new clients was that, regardless of the financial products, some clients would cease investing in their product(s) when money was tight.

They would treat it just like any other bill because they never fully grasped the overall purpose behind it in the first place. It's a clear case of being persuaded into something rather than choosing it explicitly.

FINANCIAL EDUCATION USED AS A SALES TACTIC

In today's age, customers need to be even more careful because most banks, insurance companies, and securities firms use "financial education" as a tool to sell more financial products.

Thus, some financial companies take advantage of their potential clients' apparent lack of understanding and use financial education to market complex financial products to consumers.[61]

They are able to do this because those who enroll in personal finance courses can succumb to poor financial choices because of their lack of mindfulness toward money.

It's as though the lack of financial education presents an opportunity for financial institutions to promote "financial education" to those who are vulnerable to accept any information as truth.

In this environment, you can be sold into applying for something that may come across as beneficial when you first learn about it, but after a few months, you may not even remember its purpose, or get the results you were expecting.

However, who can you turn to if you are earnestly searching for a financial company to give you answers? It can be a dicey situation if you don't yet know how to take charge of your own financial awareness.

Become The Financial Guru For Yourself

By now, you understand that everyone in the financial industry is trying to profit from you. It's their job. Perhaps you could cut them some slack and realize it's probably not their fault because they are only working as they've been trained.

Financial agents do what they're trained to do or what would earn them a few extra bucks to feed their family. The point here is to understand that you should not shy away from researching and taking advantage of any opportunities you come across. Just make sure to do the research necessary to help you make sound financial choices.

If you think you have no financial knowledge and no clue about how to save for retirement or avoid the hurdles of your financial growth, you need to start learning.

You don't need an agent. There is plenty of information you can find out online.

When you do things independently, you become an expert of your own in a matter of time. Personal finance has to be your passion project in life. The more you make an effort to build your knowledge and expertise, the fewer mistakes you'll make and the better hold you'll gain on your finances.

I soon realized that competing to get clients into products was not helping if my clients (nor I) still did not understand how to use money at a fundamental level.

LEARNING ON MY OWN

The only way I could learn what I needed to know was to get out of the industry I worked for, and leave the agency I had built up over the years.

I finally decided to branch out on my own.

This was important for my growth because while working within the industry, I knew only about the policies or products I was offering.

I couldn't spend much time exploring what other companies were up to. It was taboo to visit other competitors' offices/websites to research. My knowledge was limited to what I learned within my company.

After I walked away, I had a lot more free time on my hands, so I went to the library and made a concerted effort to read everything I could get my hands on within the subject of finance—books by Warren Buffet, Howard Marks, John Bogle, and more.

Through these books, I realized I didn't honestly know how stocks worked, or how various investment strategies applied to different investors based on their age, or how buying assets fit into retirement, or many other similar subjects.

Some of the subjects I started diving into included stocks, real estate, life insurance, financial planning, trusts, and passive income.

After 5+ years of research and testing, I learned something very intriguing about the money game.

It's not about products...

It's about a system!

This was very interesting for me, as my years of financial training caused me to believe that winning the financial game was about the specific products you use.

I thought it was about which product was cheaper. Or which product gave the better returns. Or which product would provide the best payouts at retirement age.

But winning the money game is not about products at all.

It's about having a system you deploy that will help you to win the money game on a weekly, monthly, and annual basis.

Through this information, I've uncovered the G.A. Money System, which will help you defeat all three money villains, and move you ahead financially in a simple format that anyone can follow.

In the following chapters, we will explain how to defeat each of the money villains systematically.

Please turn to the next page, and let's start with the first one...

CHAPTER 6
DEFEATING THE FIRST VILLAIN

"Do not save what is left after spending; instead, spend what is left after saving."

— WARREN BUFFETT

Concerns around money don't have to be as frustrating as they are depicted in the media. We all have the ability to raise our financial vibration. You can feel empowered about your finances, even as a teenager or a young adult.

You don't have to feel bogged down by student loans, credit cards, or other forms of debt. A simple shift in mindset can free up your energy around debt. The choice of using your mind to think in this certain way is up to you.

If you spontaneously spend everything you earn each month without any budget or proper financial planning, it's a recipe for a debt-ridden life. Thus, you need to have a system in place —a way to stay away from bad debt and have more of your income secured to allow it to flourish.

So let's unveil the first pillar of the G.A. Money System—a simple, yet profound method to keep your finances in good shape. The earlier you learn about it, the wiser you will be in dealing with emergencies, investing, debt management, and other money matters.

It would be best if you got this basic idea entrenched in your subconscious right now. There is no use in trying to grasp more advanced money lessons before this first step becomes second nature in your financial journey.

You need to understand how to systematically build up a cash reserve, which will help you take care of the first money demon —mindless debt.

Debt can behave as a psychological threat to your financial goals.

For some people, debt keeps them distressed and pulls them away from the sustained pursuit of any significant financial achievement. Thus, it would be best if you got it under control before you take steps toward more complex financial planning.

There is a discouraging money mindset that is prevalent in those who are not familiar with financial freedom. This is the belief that saving is "too hard" or they don't have enough to save.

These people have an idea that they will start saving "later". They will wait until when times are better for them to start saving; for example, when they get a raise at work. "As soon as I finish paying down my car note, then I'll start saving," Or, "I need to use all my money for gas right now. As soon as gas prices go down, then you bet! I'll be saving loads of money after that!"

People with this mentality miss out on the simplicity of wealth creation.

You don't have to do something incredibly hard to get rich. It's not about a lucky day. It's simple. Simple doesn't mean it's easy. Simple doesn't mean it's what everyone else around you is doing.

Defeating the first villain in the money game can be accomplished through a determined and consistent habit of saving that will build your financial freedom from the ground up.

ANCIENT LESSONS DISCOVERED

To help you understand the power of saving, I'd like to tell you about one of the best books I discovered on my journey when I ventured out on my own.

The book is called *The Richest Man In Babylon*, first published in 1926, almost 100 years ago.

This book is based on financial principles passed down by the ancient Babylonians.

These financial principles are literally over 1000 years old!

The ancient Babylonians were known to be one of the wealthiest societies in the history of our civilization, and there's a reason behind it. They believed in making wise choices quickly and building wealth over time.

Money Lessons From the Book

The book has quite a few great money lessons everyone should know about. These lessons are precious to young adults who are still breaking into their tender financial lives. However, these principles can be applied to people of any age, economic background, or culture.

For those who have never read the book, and also for those who have read the book before, but forgot what was inside, here are a couple of my favorite takeaways:

- Spend cautiously by differentiating between your needs and wants,
- Don't leave all your money in your savings account– Make it work for you,
- Be aware of anything that promises quick returns because there's nothing like "get rich quick"; People attain wealth with patience, consistent effort, and knowledge,

- Think of ways to make more money, develop new skills, or brush up on what you already know,
- Don't put your money into something you don't understand or know little about...

...and so forth. There are many great foundational principles in this book.[62]

One of the most respected figures in the book is Arkad, who teaches financial principles throughout the country.

One day, a student asks Arkad how he became the wealthiest man in Babylon.

RAGS-TO-RICHES STORY OF ARKAD

In response to the student's question, Arkad told the story of how he started in very humble beginnings, working as a stone mason. Specifically, Arkad would carve inscriptions upon stone tablets based on patrons' requests.

This was laborious work, as you can imagine. And there were not many employees who worked with Arkad to help ease the burden when there was a lot of work to be done.

One day, a particularly difficult task was given to Arkad, and work was commanded to be finished by the end of the day. Even though Arkad carved on the stone tablets all day, he could not finish the job in time.

The customer came back to the store to find the work unfinished. The customer was a very wealthy man, and he was extremely upset at Arkad. So Arkad made him a deal.

"I will agree to work on your tablets all night long until the job is finished, and have your tablets done by sunrise, if you will tell me the secret to being wealthy," Arkad wagered.

The wealthy customer balked for a second, but thought it was admirable of this poor stone carver to make such a bold offer for an exchange of knowledge. So the wealthy man agreed.

Arkad slaved away on the tablets all night long, and the sun was coming up by the time he finished. In the morning, Arkad felt excessively sleep-deprived, and his hands were bleeding from the amount of sweat equity he put into the project.

As soon as the shop opened for business, the rich customer entered, ready to berate the stone worker if the work was not completed again...

But surprisingly, the customer entered the store to find his rush order completed as promised, and the duty was fulfilled.

"Now, give me what you promised me, sir!" Arkad asked, bloody and exhausted.

"Very well," began the customer. "A part of all you earn is yours to keep."

"That's it?" asked Arkad.

"It was enough to turn a humble sheepherder into one of the wealthiest moneylenders in the city," the man responded.

"But everything I earn is mine to keep, isn't it?" Arkad refuted.

"No, fool..." The customer started in.

"You must pay to get your clothes sewn, so the seamstress gets a piece. You have to pay the goat herder for the milk you drink, so the goat herder gets a piece. You must pay for meats from the butcher, so he gets a piece. You must pay the tax to the lord of your land, so he gets a piece, too. You have to pay to wine and dine that lady (or fellow) of yours to keep them happy, so all of those entertainment centers you visit get a piece... But remember, before you pay any of them, a part of everything you earn is YOURS to keep!"

Arkad's implementation of this man's teaching directly led him to become the richest man in Babylon.[63]

I indulged in the story a bit, and my rendition doesn't quite sound like the one in the original book. That's how it sounded to me when I read it. But it's a beautiful book, a speedy read, and highly recommended. You will get many simple insights that will sustain you throughout your financial journey.

In Arkad's Rags-to-Riches story, the fact we need to take away is that the money we earn doesn't automatically stay with us. We must give it away to different people regularly—the landlord, grocery store, utility company, and various other merchants.

The money has to go out of your pocket for you to survive. However, if you don't prioritize the portion of the money that goes to yourself, and only focus on the money going to everyone else, that's no good.

You're skipping the most important payment. Your money will be constantly directed toward everyone else in perpetuity. Very rarely will anything ever be left over for you.

Remember, Arkad was a simple man with no special skills or background, yet he managed to acquire wealth in a manner that nobody could imagine because he sought advice from the right source.

For myself, this lesson became the foundation for me to go from having very little money saved and no money invested, to having a lot of money saved and growing my first significant investments.

As another bonus, I am giving you an audio-recorded reading of my favorite chapter of the *Richest Man In Babylon* as a gift when you visit: *www.101moneysecrets.com/listen*

WHO GETS PAID FIRST?

Another way of stating this teaching is to "Pay Yourself First".

Before you pay others for their livelihood, pay yourself first.[63]

Make it a rule to set aside no less than 10% of your earnings. If you are inspired to pay yourself more, that's fine, but 10% is a perfect amount to develop the habit.

Whether you get paid weekly or monthly, do this first thing first, and save a tenth of your earnings. If you're self-employed and not on a fixed income, you still need to pay yourself first whenever money comes in.

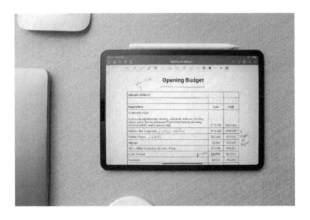

As you set aside this portion, you'll realize that you can get through the month with very little difference. You'll actually forget you're living on 90%; it won't feel any different than before.

It will become easier to develop this habit as you realize that a portion of the money entering your account will always belong to you.

This will help you appreciate the money that comes to you even more. You will start to realize that a piece of every dollar you receive will actually be yours.

Just imagine if you had been doing this for the past five years... How much cash reserves would you have right now? This is money that would be yours to keep.

The mustard seed is tiny when sown, but when you nurture it patiently, it grows into a huge tree that bears fruit for you.

The principle of money is the same. You need to be diligent about sowing the seeds of saving and allowing them to grow. Once the money tree is grown and bearing fruit, you can put the fruit to labor for you and make it multiply.

The best way to pay yourself first is to make it automatic. Set up an auto transfer for at least 10% of your monthly earnings to be moved into a separate account. This is a great way to be disciplined and consistent with saving. Before long, you will notice the money you're setting aside swelling to a level you will be excited about.

Paying yourself first can be better than other saving methods because it eliminates the constant worry about overspending. If you've saved 10% or more from your income, you can spend the rest any way you like.

There's no overspending with this method, because the goal is saving money, and you already took care of that at the very beginning. If you manage to have anything leftover from the remaining 90%, it's a bonus.

This tool helps tremendously to increase the amount of money you have for yourself, and allows you to spend money freely without worrying about blowing through all your cash reserves.

SUCCESSFULLY BUILDING YOUR EMERGENCY FUND

Next, allow the cash to build up until you have an emergency fund of at least three to six months worth of monthly expenses saved. When building a concrete financial foundation, you'll want to have the security of a protective shield for yourself in case of anything unexpected.[64]

The money you have set aside for emergencies provides backing for you in case something unpredictable happens, and you're unable to earn. The coronavirus proved that life could turn upside down with no prior warning or signal.

Having this lump sum of cash gives you peace of mind that you will be prepared to face the worst and come out of it safely.

You can calculate your emergency fund based on your monthly wages or your expenses. The recommended option is to save three to six months' worth of your household expenses. So even though you earn $2,000 a month, you should save the average amount you actually spend each month. If you haven't kept track of your monthly expenses, it's time to do that now.

You can start by getting all the monthly bills together and considering how much you spend on rent, groceries, eating out, commuting, and all sorts of fixed and discretionary expenses. Try to overestimate these expenses slightly to give yourself a buffer.

Once you have a record of your expenses in the last few months, you can come up with an average number that you'll want to multiply by three. For instance, if your monthly expenses total roughly $1,500, you should save a minimum of $4,500 as your emergency fund.

The average person will keep this simple expenses exercise on the back burner, thinking that a lump sum of cash will eventually fall into their pocket from the sky. The average person wishes they could walk down the street and trip over a briefcase filled with thousands of dollars. The average person prays for bank errors, like how the woman in Texas accidentally had $37 Million deposited in her bank account.[65]

Unfortunately, this isn't a game of monopoly, friend. Bank errors don't just happen in your favor. And if they do, the banks are taking that money back immediately (just ask the woman in Texas).

It's time for you to take control of your personal finances, and that starts with a habit. This habit will lead to you having a lump sum of cash. This lump sum of cash will give you greater financial peace of mind.

Emergency Fund's Purpose

Also, make sure that you stay disciplined and realize your emergency fund's purpose. There is a difference between a luxury (you really want it) and an emergency (you have no choice).

As your emergency fund grows, you may be tempted to deplete the funds on something unnecessary. Watch this urge, and stay true to the vision of living in financial ease.

If you need to take an impromptu trip somewhere, don't take money from your emergency savings. You may want to cancel or postpone some of your other discretionary expenses to make money available for any unplanned expenditures.

Once you have built this savings amount the first time, it becomes easier to build it the second time. And even easier the third time. Eventually, having money will become second nature to you.

Keeping Your Emergency Fund Liquid

You should also remember to keep your emergency fund liquid, which means it should be readily accessible.

It makes no sense to have a vast amount of money saved and not be able to withdraw it when an emergency arises. The purpose of an emergency fund is to provide quick cash when the unexpected happens. Thus, you should keep your emergency fund in a savings or checking account.

This should be a separate account, so you don't accidentally mix it with your spending money and give yourself the false perception that this is the same as your everyday cash.

Suppose you don't have a separate savings or checking account. In that case, you'll want to open one and transfer the determined amount every month (whenever you get paid) to accumulate the money, which will be dedicated exclusively to emergencies.

For more options, an emergency fund can be deposited into a high-yield savings account, money market account, or a Certificate of Deposit (CD), provided your bank allows you to withdraw cash in an emergency without a penalty.

You should verify if the bank has any fees associated with these accounts, and for a CD, make sure to withdraw money as the CD reaches its maturity date, or your money will be converted into a new CD.

The benefit of choosing these options is that you're likely to get a better interest rate on your funds than you get with a traditional savings or checking account.

You may also want to hide some cash in an envelope, label it as "Emergency Fund" and keep it safe. While keeping cash in an envelope might be an old-fashioned way of saving money, it can prove to be helpful when you need cash immediately. However, do your best to ensure that you only use the money when absolutely necessary.

BECOME FAMILIAR WITH YOUR SITUATION

Make the process of building your cash reserves much easier on yourself by getting familiar with your financial situation and plugging any leaks in your financial ship.[66]

DEBTS, EXPENSES, EARNINGS, AND SAVINGS

Begin by evaluating the total amount of debt you owe in totality—credit card debt, and any loans. For the credit cards you have, it's essential to write down the total balances due, the monthly payment, and the Annual Percentage Rates (APRs) you're paying on each of them.

Then tally up your average expenses per month, such as groceries, utilities, and rent.

Take a look at your total debt and total expenses compared to your total income (minus 10% for savings) and see if you're spending within your means or not.

If you're in the green, and your income can support your spending and debt payoff, then you are good to go. Simply make sure your savings are automated.

If you are in the red, and your spending/debt payoff/savings puts you in the negative when compared to your current income, then you have three options. Each one of these options can work for you:

1) Reduce Expenses,

2) Make More Money, or

3) Both

• • •

To make your financial household work for your benefit, you may have to tweak some things in your life. These are slight changes that can make all the difference for you.

You can turn a bad financial situation into a manageable one, or even a great one, with little physical effort. Most of the changes you must prepare for are the mental changes you need to cultivate.

The first mental shift relates to your discretionary expenses.

Now that you have calculated all your expenses, which expense(s) stick out to you as something that can be eliminated, reduced, or paused for a few months?

Whatever those items are, make them the first priority to take care of. Take the actions necessary to eliminate, reduce, or pause those spending activities. As soon as you do that, your income instantly goes further for you.

Other things which may not be as obvious is shopping at a cheaper store, like Dollar Tree, to save money. You may also use certain cashback portals to shop and receive cashback for purchases. Or you can find special coupons that will give you steep discounts for the items you buy every month.

If you are still in the red after reducing your expenses, you can move to the second mental shift, which is earning discretionary income.

Realize there are many methods you can use to earn extra income every month.

Besides working an extra job, which is an obvious solution, there are multiple ways to earn extra income at home, simply using your smartphone or laptop.

For example, you could sign up to participate in focus groups. Most focus groups are conducted by phone interviews, last about an hour, and pay you handsomely for your time.

Or you could earn extra money by simply watching videos and getting paid to share your opinion on the video. Or you could make extra money by filling out online surveys. Or downloading apps to your phone and testing them out for a few minutes.

Or... Or... Or...

There are countless ways to earn extra income every month.

If you haven't got your bonuses yet, go to www.101MoneySecrets.com to get 50+ ways to both reduce expenses and earn extra money.

As far as reducing expenses are concerned, you may want to make a list of all your daily expenses and make a budget. If you can stick stringently to that list, you will pay off all your debt sooner and more efficiently.

FOCUS ON ONE DEBT AT A TIME

When you decide to pay off all your debt, do it systematically and try to get rid of high-interest debts first. Pay at least the minimum due before each month's due date without fail.

It may seem overwhelming to pay off multiple debts at once. Thus, don't worry about all the debts. Send each debt the minimum payment, and focus your efforts on putting your extra money into one debt at a time (more on that later).[67]

You may need to stop using your credit cards entirely for a few months until you get this high-interest debt under control. During this time, use cash to curb spending.

If you don't change your ways, you'll never surpass the first-level money villain. The worried mindset of being riddled with debt can be overwhelming when combined with other pressures that we have to face in life.

Let's put this behind us once and for all.

The good news is the main changes we have to make to get past this are mental shifts.

The root cause of debt is usually the wrong money mindset and bad spending habits.

Therefore, eliminating debt is equivalent to developing a new mindset and implementing new money habits to sustain the financial lifestyle we desire.

DEBT REPAYMENT STRATEGIES

While building your emergency fund, you can also get out of high-interest debt or unnecessary debt. Debt repayment is much easier when done strategically, so here are a few strategies you can explore:

- Pick the credit card with the highest interest rate, and pay it off first.
- People usually pay just the minimum, thinking that it's easier, and you can continue to use your credit card; however, when you pay just the minimum, it takes longer to pay off the card because of the accrued interest. The smarter thing to do is to pay much more than the minimum, as it will reduce the overall interest you'd be paying.
- If you have multiple high-interest balances to pay off, you should consolidate all your debt into one and pay them all off together with a lower rate of interest. This will help you pay down your debt faster, and you may be more motivated after your numerous accounts get reduced to one.
- Look for balance transfer offers to move your high-interest cards to a lower APR. You can take advantage of introductory rates of 0%, where you're usually allowed to make a balance transfer within the first 12 or 18 months. Many times there is a fee for this, sometimes not.
- You can also utilize your home's equity to pay down some of your high-interest debt. It may give you a lower interest rate than the current rates you have.
- You may also seek help from a nonprofit credit counseling agency if you owe too much debt with

high APRs. They may be able to set up a suitable repayment plan for you and reduce the interest rates.

DEBT REPAYMENT METHODS

Another way to accelerate debt repayment is to experiment with the Avalanche or the Snowball Methods. Both techniques work well with consumer debts, such as student loans, personal loans, car loans, medical bills, and credit card balances.[66]

Here is a brief example of how to apply these methods to pay off multiple debts at once:

THE SNOWBALL METHOD

The snowball method helps you to get rid of the smallest balance first and keep the highest balance to be paid off at the end.

With this strategy, you don't necessarily need to worry about the interest rate on your balances. All you need to do is rank your debts in the order of the lowest balance to the highest balance and start directing extra money toward the lowest balance, making only minimum payments on all other balances.

For example, suppose you owe a total of $1,000 on one credit card (with a minimum due of $50), $1,500 on another credit card (with a minimum due of $65), and $2,000 on a student loan (with a minimum payment requirement of $100). In that case, you'll focus on repaying the $1,000 credit card as a priority because it has the lowest balance.

And let's say you've decided to use $500 each month toward your entire debt repayment, you can make the minimum monthly payments on the two higher debts, while allocating the remaining $335 toward the lowest balance.

Once the $1,000 balance is paid in full, you can restructure your payments to prioritize the second balance, and pay $400 towards that one (keep paying the minimum on the third) until the second debt is repaid.

Then after the first two debts are paid, you will pay the full $500 debt payment to the third debt until that one is wholly paid.

The snowball method will help you build momentum in your debt payments while picking up easy wins along the way. After you've paid off the smallest debt, it will instill confidence in you to pay off other debts.

You can apply this repayment technique to all kinds of debt (personal loans, car loans, student loans, medical bills, and credit cards).

However, you should choose your debt repayment amount based on your unique financial situation. Make sure that the sum you use to repay your loans doesn't prevent you from taking care of your other expenses like your house rent, groceries, utilities, and other mandatory expenses.

It's also recommended that if you have a similar remaining balance on two loans, and are not sure which order to pay them off, try to pay off the one with the higher interest rate first.

For instance, if you have a balance of $5000 on a credit card with an interest rate of 18%, and a $5000 balance on an auto loan with an interest rate of 5%, you can prioritize paying off the credit card first, since it has the higher interest rate.

The Avalanche Method

The avalanche method aims to get rid of the debt with the highest interest rate first and make only minimum payments toward the other debts. After you pay off the debt with the highest interest rate, you work your way down to paying off the debts with lower interest rates.

It doesn't matter how much your balance is on a particular credit card or a loan; this method is all about the interest rate.

Using the above example, you've decided to allocate $500 each month from your paycheck toward debt repayment, and the minimum due on each debt adds up to $215. You have two credit cards, owing $1,000 on one card, which has an APR of 10%; $1,500 on the second card, which has an interest rate of 17%, and a student loan of $2,000 with an interest rate of 12%.

With the avalanche method, you will maximize your payments toward the second credit card. You will pay the minimum balance on the other two debts, while paying $335 out of the $500 toward the second card, as it has the highest APR.

Once you've completely paid off the second card, you'll move on to repaying the second highest-interest debt (the student loan), and then the final debt with the lowest interest rate.

After you've paid off the first debt, you use the extra funds to accelerate the repayment of the second debt, and so on.

By prioritizing the highest APR debt, you'll be able to reduce the overall interest you are paying on the debts. This strategy reduces the overall interest you are paying. However, the first debt may take a little longer to pay off, as it may not be the smallest amount.

It's a good idea to set up automatic minimum payments on all debts, so you can relax knowing that you will fulfill all your payments on time and never incur any late fees.

Keep in mind that both methods will be even more effective when you cease using the credit cards you are paying off. Switch to cash for a while until you get the debts under control.

GOOD DEBT VS. BAD DEBT

Debt management is much easier when you can differentiate between good and bad debt. Most young adults aren't aware that there's such a thing as "good debt." People are either too deep in debt, or they consider all debt to be evil.

Let's rethink debt for a minute: Debt is made to facilitate your life.

For 99% of the population, if there was no option to take out a loan, it would be nearly impossible to purchase a home with cash savings only.

Without debt, business owners would be unable to scale their companies, as there would be no loans available to help them hire more staff, buy inventory, or invest in a professional marketing campaign.

Debt is a tool that can be used to accelerate growth.

Any debt that helps you improve the quality of your life, or accelerate your development, is a good thing. Of course, you need to have a repayment plan in place before you even decide to choose debt.

If you have no clue about how you're going to repay a loan, it could work against you.

For instance, if you take out a loan to set up a restaurant, you should have a plan to pay back the loan with the revenue generated, and you should also know your repayment strategy in case your business fails.

Handling debt requires discipline and realistic expectations.

When people begin to treat debt like indefinite interest-free loans, and forget that it needs to be paid back, they get into the problematic debt cycle. This is most common with credit cards and student loans.

With credit cards and student loans, we usually receive an interest-free period with no payments or low minimums for months or years. It's easy to forget about it until debt payments increase dramatically and the interest-free period ends. Many times, the first late payment will come as a surprise.

Instead of paying these debts off immediately, our poor planning can lead us to carry the balance for months or even years, costing additional interest each month.

The worst part is that we often forget what the initial debt was even used for. This is because we go into debt without having an exact plan of how we will use it for our financial benefit.

If you simply buy a watch or a pair of expensive shoes with your credit card, but don't have an established behavior of paying the card back, it's bad debt.

Similarly, taking out a loan to buy a car can be considered bad debt if you don't have a solid foundation for repayment, and the knowledge of how you will be able to consistently make the payments over time.

However, if you buy a car with the idea of renting it out for extra income, this might prove to be good debt because it will earn you money.

As a young adult, be aware of the kind of debt you choose and precisely what you will do with it. The best approach to debt is to know your purpose behind applying for credit cards and loans.

If the purpose is for your benefit and growth, and if you have a strategy to pay it back, go for it.

If you want to go into debt to buy the latest shoe drop, but you don't know how/when you'll have the money to pay it back, consider saving up the cash to buy the shoes first before putting it on the credit card. This way, you have the assurance that the cash in the bank is already available to pay back the credit card when the due date comes.

When you learn to use credit cards in this manner, you can borrow money off your credit card for short periods of time, and you will incur no interest charges if you use the credit card during the grace period (bonus tip).[68]

Getting out of debt is a simple process for someone with a positive financial outlook. If you think long-term and dream of creating a meaningful life, you will get out of debt.

It's just about staying focused and being determined about your goals.

Besides the repayment methods, developing a sound savings habit will help propel your financial independence. It's better to sacrifice a few momentary pleasures of today for the sake of savoring the meaningful accomplishments of tomorrow.

Once we have the first money villain (mindless debt) under control, we can take on the second money villain, taxes.

CHAPTER 7

SLAYING THE TAX DRAGON

*"Think of discomfort as currency- it's the price you
pay to learn some pretty crucial things."*

— LILLY SINGH

Now that you've discovered how to eliminate the mindless debt that's been dragging down your financial peace of mind, we can deflate the second money pitfall— Taxes.

As mentioned in chapter two, the average person loses 44 cents of every dollar before it's spent. When taxes are not kept in check it can affect both high-income and low-income alike.

However, the good news is that you can reduce your tax burden (legally) to a great extent. Defeating this money villain first starts with awareness, and then taking the necessary actions to improve.

There are tax-saving strategies that anyone can use for themselves, regardless of income level. Let's discuss a few of the strategies below.

CLAIM DEDUCTIONS AS A SELF-EMPLOYED INDIVIDUAL

One of the easiest ways to reduce your tax burden is to start a home-based business and claim deductions for all your business expenses.[69]

As a business owner, you will have necessary start-up costs to get the business off the ground, and ongoing costs to run the business.

Here's an idea of the deductions you can claim:

- Postal expenses,
- Gas to drive to business meetings,
- Internet service,
- Business clothing,
- Membership fees,
- Office supplies,
- Office space (home office) rent/utilities, and
- Any other business-related costs that you have.

Another great way to save on taxes is to synchronize your personal and business travel.

For instance, the next time you book a personal holiday, you can reduce the trip's expenses by focusing a portion of your trip on business activities.

This will allow you to reduce your vacation expenses by writing off a percentage of the trip you spent conducting business activities. This includes airfare, hotels, food, transportation, etc.

Be sure to consult a tax professional to do this correctly.

You get many more tax breaks as a self-employed business owner. And you don't need an LLC or any particular Corporation registered in your name to do this.

Remember, businesses start from an idea. Some entrepreneurs work in business for themselves for years without any special documents or even a business name. Simply find something you are interested in, possibly a side hustle you are already working on, and declare yourself a businessperson.

And if there is nothing you have been working on now, and you are not sure how to legitimately go into business (in a more tangible way), consider becoming an independent consultant for one of the dozens of network marketing companies, like MaryKay or Amway.

As another idea, when you read the "How To Earn Money" section in 101 Money Secrets, you can choose one of the methods mentioned to make money, and begin to write off any expenses you incur as a result of regularly performing the money-making activities.

The tax deductions you will receive as a businessperson cannot be understated. There are so many tax deductions that business owners themselves may not fully be aware of all of them[70]. Other business expenses you can write off:

- Business cards,
- Website Costs,
- Hiring Marketing Expert(s)
- Marketing software,

- Educational Events/Courses,
- Bookkeeping,
- Tax Preparer fees,
- Accounting software,
- Business Cell Phone,
- Etc.

You need to be proactive about recognizing and monitoring your tax-deductible business expenses to gain the maximum tax deduction every year. This will help you reduce your tax burden dramatically.

TAX-SAVING STRATEGIES FOR HIGH INCOME

Suppose you fall into the high-income bracket, and need a slightly more advanced strategy to reduce your tax burden. In that case, you can follow the example of the wealthiest individuals and form a 501(c)(3) nonprofit organization.

START A NON-PROFIT FOUNDATION

Increasingly, the ultra-rich, celebrities, and CEOs of big companies establish their own charitable foundations to save taxes. They donate a certain portion of their gross yearly earnings to their own foundations, which is a tax deduction.

Generally, foundations must distribute at least five percent of their net income to charity each year. That's just $5,000 out of every $100,000 received.

The wealthy individuals who figure this out can create an even larger tax break by making the contribution to a donor-advised fund run by a community foundation. These types of funds do not have any minimum requirement of a yearly donation to charity.[71]

There is nothing sinister about these methods. They are absolutely legal methods to reduce your tax exposure. If you know about these rules, you can play the money game smarter if/when you decide to keep more than 56 cents of each dollar.

Remember to consult a licensed professional to understand the ins and outs if this relates to you.

Charitable organizations may claim many tax deductions, similar to businesses.[72]

These tax deductions include:

- Maintenance costs (repair work)
- Wages and Health benefits for staff
- Hiring contractors for jobs
- Organization-related travel for members of the team, including Board Members
- Marketing expenses, including print and digital advertising
- Community events
- Staff training programs
- Office Rent
- Expenses related to property acquisitions
- And many, many more!

Not to mention, nonprofit foundations' Chief Executive Officers (CEOs) get paid handsomely, and their salaries qualify as a tax deduction.

When collecting data on Nonprofit CEO compensation, the median salary is $132,739.

Interestingly, a survey found that the higher the foundation's tax deduction, the higher the CEO's salary.[73]

It's all about knowing the rules of the game!

TAX-SAVING STRATEGIES FOR EVERYONE

For those without either high income or a side business, there are still ways you can reduce your tax burden today.[69]

Open An IRA, 401k, And/Or Roth

Save on taxes by starting a retirement account, such as a 401(k) or IRA. It's a tax-saving tactic that anyone can use, and it's widespread and easily accessible.

Your contributions toward your workplace 401(k), and IRA accounts, will reduce your taxable income and lower your tax bill.

The best part is that the funds you transfer into these accounts can mature tax-deferred until you are ready to withdraw (preferably between $59^{1/2}$ and $70^{1/2}$).

Apart from traditional retirement accounts, there are Roth accounts that you can apply for. However, the tax savings happen a bit differently in Roth accounts. You do not get a tax deduction today for money you put into the Roth; however, you get tax-free growth on your funds and do not have to pay taxes when you withdraw (between $59^{1/2}$ and $70^{1/2}$).

While your contributions to a 401(k), or traditional IRA, do help you cut down on paying taxes today, you are still liable to pay taxes on distributions. Thus, you may pay a more significant amount in the future once you are ready to use the funds, assuming your account value grows.

Since Roth contributions are funded with net income, there are no tax deductions that take place. Be aware that your contributions to a Roth IRA (or Roth 401(k)) do not reduce your gross income. The real benefit is that when you retire and want to withdraw your money, there is no tax obligation on you.[74]

START A HEALTH SAVINGS ACCOUNT (HSA)

Another useful tax-saving method is a Health Savings Account (HSA), which is suitable for someone on a qualified high-deductible medical plan. When you contribute toward an HSA, you get an instant tax deduction.

This means the money you spend on medical bills, or any medical need, is not taxed. This will reduce your tax exposure for any health expenses.

The money you contribute accumulates tax-deferred, but can be withdrawn tax-free as long as the expenses you declare are valid medical costs.

You can still use the money for non-medical (or non-eligible) expenses, but just be prepared to pay taxes on the money.

AMERICAN OPPORTUNITY TAX CREDIT (AOTC) FOR COLLEGE Students

If you're a student, you can take advantage of the American Opportunity Tax Credit (AOTC), which is meant to exempt you from taxes for eligible education expenses.

This tax credit can be availed if you're enrolled in college, and will grant you up to $2,500 per year (for four years).

Also, it can be used by a dependent or your spouse as long as they're paying for their college education. Each qualified student can get the maximum annual credit of $2,500.

Also, parents can claim a bonus tax credit of $2,500 if they currently pay for their child's schooling. This doesn't only have to be a college or university, by the way. Any vocational school or other post-secondary educational institution also counts.

If the credit you receive exceeds your taxable amount, you may even get a tax refund.

Qualify For An Earned Income Tax Credit

The Earned Income Tax Credit (EITC) is a unique tax credit based on your income and the number of family members you have.

It's designed for low or average income earners and couples, especially those with children. If you qualify, the IRS will give you a tax credit of up to $6700+.

If you're eligible for the EITC, you may get your money back at tax filing, or receive an exemption to reduce your federal taxes. If you don't owe any federal income taxes, you can claim a refund from the government.

Deduct Mortgage Insurance Premiums

You can also deduct your mortgage insurance premiums as a homeowner.

You need to have private mortgage insurance and, if you're eligible, you can deduct the mortgage insurance premiums as an itemized deduction on your tax return.

However, you cannot claim this deduction if your Adjusted Gross Income (AGI) is $109,000 or higher (for 2021).

The qualifications are subject to change. Please look into this yourself if you are a homeowner and think you may qualify.

Invest In Opportunity Zones Or Opportunity Funds

Opportunity Zones, or Opportunity Funds, are another way to save enormous sums on taxes.

Opportunity Zones are certain geographic regions that are recognized as economically stagnant. They are usually distressed areas. Thus the investors who put their money into developing such areas get an incentive of tax deferment and/or significantly decreased capital gains taxes.

An Opportunity Fund is an investment instrument specifically tailored to allow investors to bet on all of the aforementioned opportunity projects at once. For example, you could invest in a business development project within an opportunity zone, and become more like an angel investor.

Beware, the economic regulations in opportunity zones may differ from those in other areas of the country or state. And many opportunity funds are only accepting accredited investors who meet specific income requirements.

WRAPPING IT ALL UP

This was a great headstart on reducing your tax burden, and this is only the first step.

The more you learn, the better you will get at reducing your tax burden, and you will learn to get creative at reducing your tax exposure in a meaningful way.

Remember, if you choose to stay unaware and don't fully capitalize on the rules of the money game, no one can help you. It's essential to know the mechanisms you can take advantage of to maximize your potential for financial growth.

In the next chapter, we will dive deeper into the third money villain—inflation—and give you a strange, but powerful technique to put yourself ahead of this wealth destroyer once and for all.

CHAPTER 8

THE INFLATION ASSASSINATION

"If you want something you've never had,
You must be willing to do something you've never
done."

— THOMAS JEFFERSON

After tackling debt and taxes, you may think there's nothing left to worry about and that your money game is on the upswing, since you will feel much more peace and ease in your money situation.

However, this final money demon is the sneakiest of them all.

You don't even see this thief coming. You only know the villain has been there after the damage is done. That's why this is the final level of the money game.

Once you've got the first two villains under control, you can focus all your attention and energy on getting this third one under wraps.

How do you beat inflation? It seems like a puzzle, doesn't it?

If you try to save a ton of money, inflation wins because your money loses value.

If you simply spend money, inflation still wins because real wages have been decreasing over time when compared to inflation. The rising costs of goods over time translates to the money you spend affording fewer and fewer goods and services.

It seems inevitable that the prices of goods and services will continue to increase, especially when you research the true value of the dollar a century ago, versus the true value of the dollar today.

Keep in mind, you still need to make sure that you are keeping some money in your bank account for unexpected emergencies, and have the means to cover your expenses every month.

This third money villain can be considered the final level of the money game.

You may not beat this level on your first try. This is the level that you may need to test a couple times. You must examine this level critically and become familiar with the ins-and-outs.

Don't rush ahead. Take your time with this one. Dedicate yourself.

You've made it this far into the money game; you need to see what happens once you win.

So how do you beat a monster that you can't see, and don't know the damage it's doing until the damage is done?

It's not logical.

With the average, regular person's mind, you can't do it.

To beat this villain, you have to be able to think like the villain.

You must go into the monster's mind, and become the monster.

Once you merge with the villain, you'll know the tactics to defeat the villain.

Once you learn to think as the monster thinks, you find the answer to this illogical conundrum to be so obvious, you'll wonder why you never saw it before.

Unfortunately, some of the information you will read here will make no sense to the standard, rational, logical brain. This is the stage where you have to become more than you are now.

And if you feel pressured to hang onto your moral, rational thinking brain, you have to ask yourself: Do I truly want to win the money game?

If the answer is yes, then get ready to have your mind blown.

Take notes on this next part.

It's time to learn about banks...

THE BIGGEST BUSINESSES IN THE WORLD

Before we get to the tangible strategies to surpass inflation, you have to understand the truth behind how banking works.

Do you realize how massive the financial industry is? If you walk down the streets of any downtown metropolitan area and look for the most prominent building, it's most likely to be covered by the logo of a bank or an insurance company.

When Forbes puts out their list every year of the 100 largest companies, you will find the list populated by a majority of banks and insurance companies.[75]

In 2022, the Forbes list shows that 32 of the top 100 companies (in the entire world) are in banking, insurance, or some kind of financial services. And at least five of the top 10 companies are specifically big banks.

For example, the Industrial & Commercial Bank of China (ICBC) was known to be the biggest company on planet earth for 19 straight years, in terms of asset value.

The other thing that is very interesting about banks is their crucial function.

Love them or hate them, we all rely on banks.

Banks are unique in that they can continue to operate and thrive regardless of a particular country's conflict, geopolitical landscape, or crippling crisis.

Even if the money system were to collapse today, new and modern banking institutions would come into existence to complement the future of currency.

Banking existed before the dollar was created, and banking will continue to exist after the dollar is dead. That's how powerful banking is and will continue to be.

Why are we talking so much about banks? You might be wondering...

The purpose of getting acquainted with banks is to understand and develop the right mindset toward your own personal finances.

To rise above the adverse effects of inflation on your money, you'll need to start treating your money as though you were the owner of your own personal bank.[76]

BANKS DON'T MAKE MONEY BY "SAVING"

Contrary to the popular belief that the bank's mission is to "save" your money, that is not entirely true. Banks are not meant to save money.

Banks use your money to make more money.[77]

After the banks receive deposits from their creditors (You & other savers), the bank has two main objectives:

1. Loan out that money to make more money
2. Repeat

Nowhere in this process do the banks make it a priority to "save" money.

You need to understand that banks earn revenue by lending money, and they get that money from depositors who keep their cash invested in banking products.

In fact, if you go to your local bank today to withdraw a substantial amount (say $10,000 or $20,000), the bank will not have the cash readily available. They will have to call around to get the money brought to them. It can take hours or days for them to present you with the physical cash.

Why is this?

It helps to know that banks operate under a system called "fractional reserve banking," which means only a fraction of the money is required to be kept on hand from the total deposits received. However, the banks can loan up to 90% of these funds.

FRACTIONAL RESERVE BANKING

It's only mandatory for banks to keep a minor portion of deposits available for withdrawal. For example, if the bank receives a deposit of $1000, they need to keep $100 cash on hand (only 10%). But the banks can now turn around and loan up to $900 (90%).

The portion that the banks need to retain is known as "reserves", which are insured by the Federal Reserve and used by the central bank to enforce the monetary policy.

Fractional reserve banking is very common in advanced civilizations.

The purpose of the fractional reserve system is to make more capital available for loaning out to borrowers and growing the economy.[78]

The money in banks is not supposed to be idle. The money is always supposed to be put to work; thus, banks generate more money from their depositors' money by earning interest on new loans.

That's how the economy prospers, and that's why banks are the largest companies on the planet.

BANKS EARN BY LOANING MONEY

Some may find banks immoral because they give us low interest rates on our accounts in exchange for the ability to loan our money out at higher interest rates.

This is how the banks turn a profit.

When you deposit your hard-earned money with a bank, they entice you to keep money in your account by offering an interest rate of return on your cash balance. (0.01% = 7200 years to double)

However, they earn huge profits by charging hefty interest rates when they lend 90% of their depositor's money to borrowers through loans and credit cards. (12% = 6 years to double)

For instance, if you want to keep $200,000 in your savings account, the bank can take 90% of your deposit ($180,000) and loan it to a borrower on the very same day.

For round numbers, let's imagine you received a 1% interest rate on your account for keeping your money with the bank, while the bank charged an average of 8% to the amount lent to borrowers as auto loans, personal lines of credit, and mortgages.

So for your $200,000 deposit, they're supposed to give you $2,000 as interest earnings (of 1%). However, they will earn a whopping $14,400 on the $180,000 they are lending (at an average interest rate of 8%).

That means the bank earns: 14,400 - 2,000 = $12,400 in profit.

It doesn't stop there.

What is the second step for the bank in this two-step process?

That's right! Repeat the process.

So now imagine the loans are paid back, and the bank has already paid you the 1% interest. You have $202,000 in your bank account, and you decide to leave your money with the bank for another year. The bank will have all your money PLUS the additional $12,400 they can lend out.

Let's do the math—

202,000 + 12,400 = $214,400 (total amount on the bank's balance sheet)

90% of 214,400 = $192,960 (amount the bank can now lend out)

The amount of lending capital available to the bank grew from $180,000 to $192,960.

If you could learn how to use your own money similar to how the bank uses your money, your money would increase significantly with each passing year.

HUGE INTEREST RATE SPREAD

To put it simply, banks leverage the money of depositors to draw great profits from borrowers. They create an interest rate spread by the distinction between the low interest paid to their banking customers and the high interest charged to borrowing customers.[79]

Lending is a legitimate and significant revenue-earning vehicle for banks, which is why they have also come up with various financial products to boost their returns.

Most bank accounts offer less than a 1% return on your money, especially the big banks. However, online banks may offer you better rates than traditional banks because of their low overhead costs and the need to attract new customers. Remember, all banks still use your money in a similar fashion.

YIELD SPREADS EXPLAINED

The banks use your money to create a nice "spread", which helps the banks make more money. This is the primary way banks have become the world's largest companies.

So, what is a yield spread? In simple words, a yield spread is the difference between two yields (earnings). It's a method to know the value/price of two debt instruments and calculate the difference.[80]

For example, if a particular bond has a yield of 10% and another one delivers 8%, the difference is 2%, which is the spread.

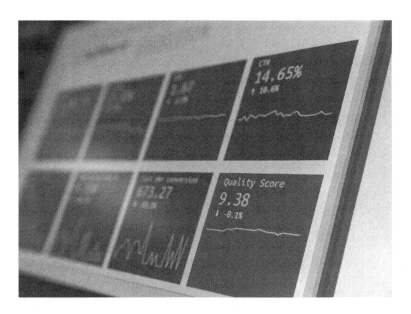

MIMIC WHAT THE BANKS ARE DOING

Therefore, the intelligent thing to do is to mimic the banks by using our money similar to how they use our money. We're going to accomplish this by:

- Step #1 – Increasing the yield on our savings
- Step #2 – Loaning out our money to make more money

#1 — INCREASE YIELDS

As a beginner in the field of investments, you should consider financial products and assets that are relatively safe and reliable.

Remember to first build an emergency fund, as we discussed in Chapter Six. Your emergency fund should be readily accessible in case of an emergency.

However, after your emergency fund is established, you need to think long-term and find ways to multiply the 10% you are continuing to set aside for yourself.

Since money is losing its value and will continue to do so, you need to make sure you're investing in stable, high-yield instruments. The real growth in your money is not about simply stashing it somewhere, but putting it to work for you.[81]

To start, it's important to put your savings into something that will keep up with inflation. Below are some of the investment instruments that may prove to be effective:

SHORT-TERM BONDS

Short-term bonds are less volatile (than other investment options), easily accessible, and offer much better growth than a savings account. Having your money here will aid in combating inflation. Another benefit to a short-term bond is that it's less likely to be crushed by rising interest rates. As your bond matures, you can reinvest the money again. Most bonds are not subject to federal income taxes.

INDIVIDUAL STOCKS

Investing money in the stock market can be one of the best ways to beat inflation. When you buy a stock, it means you become a shareholder of a company, and you share a small portion of its earnings and assets. Thus, you make a profit when the company's share price increases. Also, if the company loses value and the stock price drops, you lose money as a shareholder.

So yes, stocks can be a risky investment option if you do it without proper analysis and knowledge. Common sense says you shouldn't put your money into something you don't believe in or understand. Make sure you only invest in companies you have faith in.

TREASURY INFLATION-PROTECTED SECURITIES (TIPS)

TIPS are government securities meant to protect your money from declining purchasing power. They follow the upward and downward trend of inflation. If the inflation rate increases, the offered interest rate also goes up; similarly, with deflation, the interest rate will decline as purchasing power rises.

TIPS are a strong hedge against inflation. The best part is that you will get your original principal back at maturity. Thus, they're known to be one of the safest investments for your portfolio.

Real Estate

Investing in real estate can be profitable as long as you buy a property at the right price and wait for its value to rise. In fact, inflation can prove to be good for real estate investors if they hold property over time.

Real estate is a broad industry from an investment perspective. Thus, you need to figure out the investment strategy that is right for you. Also, most property sellers ask for large initial down payments, which prevent some people from acquiring property.

Alternatively, you can start with a Real Estate Investment Trust (REIT), which allows you to own a small portion of real estate in the form of a share. You earn dividends as your REIT portfolio earns profit from the underlying assets.

COMMODITIES

Commodity investing goes back to the ancient era when spices and silks were traded for money. In the modern age, commodities are bought and sold through mutual funds, exchange-traded funds (ETFs), and futures.

While the likelihood of profit in commodities depends largely on demand and supply, it can prove to be helpful in counteracting inflation.

The rise in prices of goods and services reflects the rise in prices of food and materials. You may invest your money in commodities to help your savings grow at the same pace.

GOLD

Buying gold can certainly prove to be a great way to diversify your investments and protect against the dollar's declining value. The value of gold, as one of the most resourceful metals, is expected to appreciate in value over time.

CRYPTOCURRENCY

Although cryptocurrencies can be highly volatile, they can grow your money exponentially over time. Cryptocurrency (crypto) is virtual currency. It requires a great understanding of how to invest here, as a simple mistake in crypto can cause a significant loss of funds. However, the entire cryptocurrency asset class (specifically bitcoin) has grown substantially faster than most investments over the same time period.

Before you start your investing journey, a word of caution: It's important to do thorough research and have a great foundational understanding of the investment before you get in.

If you want to invest in stocks, study a particular strategy you can deploy. Learn it proficiently and go into the investment with a plan. If the investment is real estate, gather information about the specific strategies available, choose the one you like best, and study it deeply before you shell out your hard-earned money.

Realize that this part of the journey will be challenging for people, as some will prefer to jump in asap and learn as they go. In fairness, it is quite possible to do a lot of research on a subject, still miss a crucial piece of information, and make a mistake that costs you money.

To curb losses, start your investment journey with amounts you can bear to lose, and as you get more experienced, add more funds.

It's better to start small, rather than go large right out of the gate and be in a state of panic if the investment doesn't work the way you expected.

Along with your bonuses, you will find the section "How To Invest" which lists over 20 resources you can use to start your investment journey. Visit www.101MoneySecrets.com.

#2 – LOAN OUT YOUR MONEY

Step #2 in defeating the third money demon is learning to lend your own money to make more money. This is a crucial piece of the G.A. Money System.

Loaning your own money doesn't necessarily mean lending money to strangers or family members (those are advanced strategies for another book).

Loaning your own money means lending money to yourself, and paying the interest back to yourself.

So, instead of paying interest to the bank, you are paying that interest back to yourself.

Sounds interesting, right? Let's dig deep into this concept.

START BY LOANING MONEY TO YOURSELF

Loaning money to yourself and paying yourself back with interest is a concept known as Infinite Banking, and is a practice that's used regularly within the most affluent families in the banking sector, such as the Rothschilds, JP Morgan, and the Rockefellers.[82]

However, this practice was brought to the public's attention when distinguished economist, Nelson Nash, revealed how it works in a book called *Become Your Own Banker*.

The unique idea is that Infinite Banking allows you to become your own bank.

One of the strategies involves the use of a dividend-yielding permanent life insurance policy. According to the concept, you can borrow from your life insurance policy's cash value and pay yourself back the same amount you would be paying to financial institutions.

Now that's an extra step, because truthfully, you don't need any unique financial product to do this. You can implement this now, for free, using only your checking or savings account.

All that is required is the discipline to pay yourself back each month like you would pay a regular bill.

If you were to google search "Infinite Banking" you would find thousands of results which all mention using life insurance as the vehicle to get this done. The reason is that when you use a life insurance policy, you receive additional perks.

Perks include:

1) The rate of return on cash-value policies will be higher than what you receive from checking and savings accounts,

2) Some cash value policies will pay regular dividends that will grow larger as you add more money to your account, and

3) Life insurance policies will have a death benefit, so when you die, your family will receive all the money, without being subject to estate taxes.

Yes, there are perks, however there are downsides if you are brand new to cash-value life insurance, and receive a policy that is not set up properly to accommodate the infinite banking model. The policy has to be set up correctly to do this, and it also has to be set up uniquely to fit your needs.

Therefore, it's better for you to realize you can start this practice now, without any special insurance product. You can do this with just a checking or savings account.

To start, you'll need a lump sum of cash (it could be $500 or $5000+, depending on where you can start).

And the next time you pay for a large expense, borrow the money from yourself instead of the bank. Then, pay yourself back in monthly installments. Use the same interest you were going to pay to the bank.

The lump sum you are using to perform this process should always be loaned out. Try not to keep the money stagnant sitting in the account. Instead, try to keep the money in circulation as much as possible. The better you get at this, the better you will improve your velocity of money, which adds more dollars to the bank account.

The best part about this strategy is that any loans you receive are 100% tax-free.

If you receive $100,000 tomorrow in the form of a loan, you do not have to pay any federal or state taxes on that. You can use this information to make your money go further (more on that later).

Once again, start this financial technique with an amount you are comfortable with. For instance, start with $500, borrow from yourself at an 8-10% interest rate, and pay yourself back monthly. Watch what happens to your account after just one year.

If you cannot figure out how to consistently pay yourself back each month, you need to go back to the first money villain, and tweak your process.

If you can't maintain payments to yourself, your foundation is weak, and you do not have the discipline to maintain significant financial success.

However, if you were to fail at any point, now is the perfect time to fail. If you come to this point, adjust your mentality, learn what you need to bounce back stronger, and hit refresh.

The better you get at this stage, the more prepared you will be to play the money game in any economic condition.

My Testimonial

Before my wife and I learned about this banking process, we were living very frugally, counting our pennies every month, and saving all our receipts (trying to defeat money villains 1 and 2).

After we started implementing this process, within one year, we both had new iPhones and MacBooks, we fixed up our home with over $35,000 worth of repairs we had been delaying, we were able to invest an extra $10,000 into our desired investments, we eliminated all our bad debts, and we acquired enough money to purchase an investment property.

It sounds unbelievable, but to top it all off, this money growth happened in the span of one year, and our household expenses stayed the same throughout the year!

These changes only happened after we learned the skills to defeat the third money villain—and we figured out how to do this during rampant inflation.

But please, don't use my example as a reason to rush your development. My situation will be very different than yours. And your situation will be quite different than your best friend's. Each situation will require a personalized approach.

The beginning stages are the most important to grow through first. Take your time with it. Get the first money villain under control, then the second, then the third.

FINAL THOUGHTS

At this point, you could be asking yourself questions like, "But how does it work?"

And as I was saying earlier in this chapter, this is not a concept that can fully be explained in one sentence, one sitting, or one book. This is a concept you will grasp over time.

That's why this third money demon is the hardest to defeat, because your brain has to become different in order to think in the ways that this third money beast thinks.

As you become well-versed in this new way of using money, your entire thought process regarding money will change.

You will no longer fear banks. You will no longer be afraid of debt. You will no longer stress over having a "perfect" amount of savings. You will no longer fear running out of money in retirement.

You will be like Neo in the movie scene when he finally became "The One".

But remember, even Neo had doubts initially and needed time to develop.

Now you have the basic overview of how to conquer the three pitfalls of wealth. We've covered a lot of subjects, and are almost ready to bring this book to a close.

BUT WAIT...

There's still one more advanced lesson that will bring this all together.

If you stop here and don't grasp the final concept, you will still be unable to put it all together.

I know everything you've read so far is more than enough to wrap your head around for most people, which is why we can only talk about one thing at a time.

If you try to implement too many things too quickly, it can backfire on you.

Going back to the basketball coaching analogy, you wouldn't want Phil Jackson to drill you on every single one of the basic basketball skills at once. You won't absorb the information very well. Even though the techniques themselves seem simple, they could be mentally exhausting,

So the final lesson in this book is the last nail in the coffin of all the money villains in one fell swoop.

This last lesson ensures that the money demons can't "rise from the dead" like Lord Voldemort did so many times in Harry Potter. This final money lesson will give you the magic spell to bind the money villains for eternity.

This advanced knowledge will elevate you above even the most credentialed financial experts. You will learn how to use your money as the wealthiest people in the world are using theirs today, including Jeff Bezos and Warren Buffet.

Once again, the next chapter will be advanced, so don't implement this until you have thoroughly researched the subject.

See you there!

CHAPTER 9

BUY, BORROW, AND THEN YOU DIE

"A national debt, if it is not excessive, will be to us a national blessing."

— ALEXANDER HAMILTON

I n the previous chapter, we introduced the two main ways you can use your money as the banks to beat inflation.

These two ways are:

1) Put your money in places to obtain higher yields, and

2) Loan your money to make more money.

The final step in the money game is to learn how to do this strategically, using leverage. There are numerous ways to do this, and no one method will be suitable for everyone.

The rich get richer because they know the importance of leverage. They have the knack for applying leverage strategically to their lives and financial situations.

The better you get at developing your own system, the quicker you will be able to live financially free with your passive income streams.

WHAT DOES "BUY, BORROW, DIE" MEAN?

"Buy, Borrow, and Die" is a phrase that came into being in the mid-1990s by Professor Ed McCaffery[83]. This strategy unravels the secret of an effective technique used by the rich.

In short, they truly understand the power of compounding wealth, and they use it to their advantage to the fullest. Your money can work and earn for you (for as long as you live), as long as you don't let it rest.

While it's important to eliminate bad debt from your life, there's a positive side to debt that can help you keep your purchasing power high (even during rising inflation) and reduce taxes significantly.

This technique will take a little bit to explain, so please be patient as you learn this strategy. It may not sound as simple as the other personal finance tips you learned earlier, so you may want to read this chapter more than once.

However, once you fully grasp this, the outcome can be absolutely monumental.

Once again, this book is not meant to give you an exact step-by-step on how to apply all the know-how to your unique situation. This book is meant to be the manual that gives you the foundation which you can build from.

HOW THE SUPER RICH AVOID PAYING TAXES

The rich continue to grow their wealth because they know how to tame, conquer, and control the three money villains: mindless debt, taxes, and inflation.

An interesting topic that comes up in the media every year or so is the idea that we should be taxing the rich at an even higher tax rate. And people become quite shocked when they find out that certain wealthy individuals like Jeff Bezos and Warren Buffet pay very little in taxes, compared to their business profits.[84]

Taxes are usually the focus because that is the only public information that most people can interpret, but that's all smoke and mirrors. You would be surprised to know that a high-level strategy is working behind the scenes, which goes beyond just taxes.

Not only do they pay very little in taxes, but they deliberately borrow money every year.

Why would a super-rich person borrow money every year instead of just using the money they already have?

Not only do they borrow money regularly and pay very little in taxes, but they also stay ahead of inflation, and actually INCREASE their purchasing power throughout the year.

This is all because they understand the power of strategically leveraging assets.

This methodology is coined the "Buy, Borrow, and Die" strategy.

"Buy, Borrow, Die" Explained

How it works is you buy an appreciating asset (it could be real estate, stocks, or a thriving business), then get a loan from the bank (borrow) using the asset as collateral.

When you get a loan against the asset, you win from the start, in a couple of ways:

1. You don't have to sell the asset (it can continue to appreciate)
2. You don't owe any taxes on a loan

This is a perfectly legal way to accelerate your financial development.

When you receive a salary (of $50,000 or $500,000), you could pay nearly 50% in income taxes. But when you receive a loan (of $50,000 or $500,000), you pay 0% in income taxes.

As an added benefit, a loan gives you access to large amounts of capital all at once. And although a salary can give you the same amount of money, it will be spread out over the entire year, which does not have the same potential as when you receive it all at once.

Another important note is this strategic debt should be used to help you make more money. After you beat money villains #1 and #2, you will know better how to handle large sums of money to your benefit. I will give an example later in the chapter.

Another enormous benefit of this strategy are the low interest rates that are charged to these types of loans.[85]

For example, the interest rate banks typically charge to loans against real estate collateral is between 1% and 5%, which is much lower than what you'll find for personal loans and credit cards.

Also, if the asset you've taken a loan against grows in value, you can use the asset to pay down the borrowed debt. Or refinance the debt and borrow more.

Suppose you happen to die with the debt unpaid. In that case, the assets can be passed onto the next generation without any tax liability by converting the asset's ownership into a charitable foundation. Find a licensed professional to help you with this.

This is just the tip of the iceberg. Want to learn more?

Keep Reading!

BORROW AGAINST STOCK PORTFOLIO

One simple example of how this strategy works is by borrowing against a stock portfolio.

You borrow money against the wealth you already have. Your wealth grows larger, since you still own the stock portfolio AND you have access to the underlying capital. It's like using your money twice. It may sound strange, but this is one of the most common ways of implementing this strategy.

According to the data given by banks, the vast majority of people using these types of loans (loans secured by portfolios of stocks and securities) are their wealthy customers.[86]

Here's how it works:

- For these loans, banks will offer low interest rates and flexible repayment terms.
- Borrowers are also eligible to obtain more cash whenever they need to (up to a limit), so they don't have to sell their stocks in unfavorable market conditions.
- The net worth of such clients is always on the rise because the growth they receive on their assets is usually higher than the rate they pay to the banks for borrowing the money.
- The customers save 100% of capital gains taxes by not selling their stocks and keeping them with the bank.
- They can access the underlying investment at any time.

SURVIVE THE DECLINE OF PURCHASING POWER

"I think I got it, Julian!" you say. "But what's the point of borrowing money? Why not just save up the cash and use the cash? And that way, we don't have to pay back anybody, right?"

That's a brilliant question! I'm so glad you asked...

Remember, this third money villain is a beast of a challenge to overcome.

Your purchasing power is getting clobbered on a regular basis.

Inflation is a giant bulldozer, and your purchasing power is a single-story wooden shed. It simply doesn't stand a chance.

The currency we use on a day-by-day basis is becoming less valuable by the day. Next month, your money will be able to buy less goods and services than the same amount of money can afford today.

How is this happening?

Let's understand the dollar's declining purchasing power with an example:

Back in 1913, $1 could buy 30 Hershey's chocolate bars.

However, if you tucked $1 between your mattress from 1913 to today, that dollar would not be able to buy the 30 Hershey's bars that it could have afforded in 1913. Today, a buck will probably get you only one Hershey's Bar (*and* you'd need a coupon).

Here's another example: In 1933, you could buy ten beer bottles for $1, but today, that same $1 can barely afford a small McDonald's coffee.

There has been a considerable shift in the number of things people could afford decades ago compared to what they can afford with the rising prices today.[87]

If we look at historical data, the U.S. dollar has been falling over the decades because of the surge in the money supply. The more dollars that get injected into circulation, the cheaper they become. And this compels you to need more dollars to buy an item today that was much cheaper before.

Our money will continue to lose its value throughout our entire life as long as we have the ability to print it out of thin air.

Thus, you need to use this information to your advantage and learn how to tactfully tip the scales in your favor!

The only way to increase and maintain your purchasing power over the years is to borrow money.

It's true!

You MUST borrow money!

Let's understand this with the help of two examples. This is where you might want to slow down and take some notes.

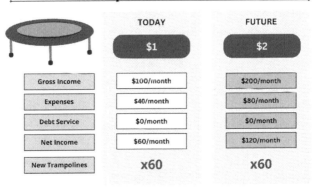

Example #1 — All Cash

	TODAY	FUTURE
	$1	$2
Gross Income	$100/month	$200/month
Expenses	$40/month	$80/month
Debt Service	$0/month	$0/month
Net Income	$60/month	$120/month
New Trampolines	x60	x60

EXAMPLE 1 – USING ALL CASH TO BUY ASSETS

WE'LL BE USING TRAMPOLINES AS AN EXAMPLE ASSET, BUT REMEMBER, the asset can be anything.

The numbers are not exactly perfect, this is just an example. However, take this to heart because this process will show you how borrowing money will improve your purchasing power.

In this first example, we will use all cash to buy an income-producing asset.

Let's imagine you buy 100 trampolines that cost only $1 each and are all generating $1 per month in revenue, totaling $100 in revenue.

The monthly expenses for maintaining the trampolines are $40/month, giving you a net profit of $60.

With this profit ($60), you can buy 60 more trampolines each month (at $1 each).

After ten years, due to inflation, the trampolines will now cost $2 each and generate $2 per month in income. The original 100 trampolines now earn $200/month in revenue.

Due to inflation, the expenses have also doubled to $80/month.

So at the end of each month, there is now a $120 profit.

End of example.

The final question is, if you were to use the $120 profit and turn around to buy more trampolines each month, how many trampolines can you afford with the $120 profit?

Remember, trampolines cost $2 each now...

Can you afford more than before? Less?

Right, it's the same.

You can still only afford 60 trampolines. Purchasing power did not change.

So you can only afford the same number of trampolines as you could back when they were $1 each. This means inflation kept you in the same spot.

Even though your profits doubled (to $120), your dollars did not go any further.

Many people have the misunderstanding that because revenue is increased, or their working wages are higher, that their purchasing power must have increased too. But inflation is a sneaky monster that will fool your logical mind.

Example #2 — All Debt

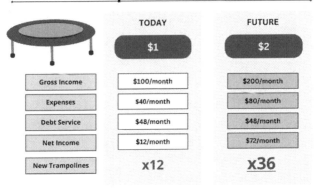

	TODAY	FUTURE
	$1	**$2**
Gross Income	$100/month	$200/month
Expenses	$40/month	$80/month
Debt Service	$48/month	$48/month
Net Income	$12/month	$72/month
New Trampolines	**x12**	**x36**

EXAMPLE 2 – USING DEBT TO BUY ASSETS

In the second example, we will start over, and purchase the same 100 trampolines at $1 each, but this time we are using ALL DEBT to buy the initial 100 trampolines.

The main difference in the second example is we now have a debt payment that needs to be satisfied each month.

So, how do the numbers work out in this scenario?

Ok, first you buy 100 trampolines.

They generate $1/month in income ($100 revenue) and have expenses of $40/month.

There is the added debt payment of $48/month.

So at the end of the month, you receive just $12 in profit and can buy 12 more trampolines.

It doesn't sound as exciting, but let's fast forward...

After ten years, the trampolines now cost $2 each and generate $2/month in income.

The original 100 trampolines earn $200/month in revenue.

The expenses have doubled to $80/month.

However, the debt payment stays the same at $48/month (we borrow money from sources that keep our borrower interest rates stable, of course).

After these calculations, you find the profit is now $72/month!

After factoring in inflation, you can purchase an additional 36 trampolines each month with your profits.

Did the purchasing power go up or down in this example?

Of course, it went way up!

Although the first all-cash example may bring more profits initially, the second all-debt scenario presents us with a 3x increase in our purchasing power over time. And purchasing power will continue to increase exponentially with each passing year, especially if we acquire more strategic debt.

Eventually, the business owner in the all-cash scenario will be out of business, because they will become stuck, feeling constrained by the lack of forward momentum.

However, the business owner in the second example will feel like they have more money than they can use, and their business is actually getting better and better. On top of that, their judicious debt management skills will cause lenders to offer them even more funding (a.k.a. debt), which could also be leveraged strategically.

It's the exact same business operation – the only difference is the first business didn't figure out how to surpass the final money villain, while the second business did!

OTHER PEOPLE'S MONEY (OPM)

Debt can be lucrative if used with a purpose.

All the big businesses, churches, governments, investors, etc., spend considerable time and effort trying to acquire OPM, which stands for "other people's money", before starting a major project.

OPM can go by names such as 'funding', 'financing', 'capital', 'grants' and more.

You may think this money grab is purely for charitable causes, or maybe you could feel it's for reasons of greed, however you may never have realized there's real wisdom behind it.

The primary way to stay ahead in the money game and retain purchasing power is to (strategically) borrow money.

So, there can be two reasons to use somebody else's money instead of your own. One, you don't have enough cash resources to buy an asset or acquire something new. Two, although you do have the cash resources, you want to use the power of strategic leverage to invest in many more assets and supercharge your purchasing power.

Taking a look at real estate as an example[88], here are multiple ways to acquire Other People's Money if you want to buy an investment property:

- *Conventional Financing*: Borrow money from a traditional financial institution like a bank or credit union. While the interest rate they offer is typically the lowest in the market, they follow strict guidelines regarding loan approval and down payment.

- **Private Money:** As the name implies, this is when you privately borrow money from somebody you know personally. The lender can be anyone (friend, relative, or colleague) besides a recognized financial institution. Since this is an informal lender, they're generally more flexible with their terms, but can charge higher interest rates. Mutual trust is the backbone of this money supply.
- **Hard Money Loan:** This is a loan given to a borrower by an individual or a company, not a bank. Hard money financing aims to carry out a short-term real estate transaction. Such a loan may cost the borrower more in terms of interest rates, but are readily available and have flexible terms compared to other loans.
- **Seller Financing:** When a real estate buyer seeks a loan from the owner of the property, it's called seller (or owner) financing. There's no conventional bank involved in the agreement, as this is carried out between the buyer and seller.
- **Partnerships:** As the name suggests, when two people decide to join together in a business deal, they form a partnership. One person can bring in their skills and expertise while the other provides the capital. They both split the profits 50/50, or whatever is agreed upon.

Some forms of OPM require no repayment, such as grants and donations. Then there are forms of OPM that allow you to defer payments for a number of months into the future, or pay extremely low interest rates, which can allow you to reduce debt expenses (also known as "debt service") even more.[89]

Borrowers can use their successful borrower history to acquire favorable terms on subsequent loans. The cheaper you can bring down your debt service, the better you can improve your purchasing power.

ASSETS YOU CAN BORROW AGAINST

If you thought the "Buy, Borrow, Die" strategy was only for the wealthy, it's time to bust the myth and unveil the truth that every person has an equal opportunity to get their personal finances under control, acquire financial assets, and reduce tax exposure by borrowing against their assets.[90]

Here are some of the assets you can use to borrow against (even if you're not a billionaire):

Brokerage Accounts

You can use half of the cash value of your investments as collateral to secure the loan.

There isn't any high fee involved in comparison to the capital gains taxes you'd have to pay on the appreciation of the securities. Also, you may find this to be a beneficial option if you consider the opportunity costs. Check with your brokerage firm and see the terms for borrowing against your investments.

Crypto Assets

You can obtain a loan against your crypto assets. There's a possibility of borrowing at 0% APR, too. However, you need to find that out with your crypto provider.

Life Insurance Policies

You can use the cash value in life insurance policies as collateral to borrow against. This is called a policy loan, and there are many famous stories of people borrowing from their policies, including Walt Disney to build Disneyland during the depression.

Real Estate

If you own a property, consider using it as collateral for a large lump sum of long-term funds at low interest rates. Most commonly, borrowers tap into their home equity through refinancing, or a home equity line of credit (HELOC).

Other Options

Then there are other assets you can leverage, such as limited partnerships, offshore corporations, and more. Loans allow you to access cash without reducing or revoking your ownership of the asset(s) or hindering the growth of your assets.

IT'S ALL ABOUT HAVING THE KNOWLEDGE

The financially savvy are able to avoid the money pitfalls because they know the tactic of tipping the odds of the money game in their favor. It's not about having great financial advisors, lawyers, and accountants.

Each individual needs to take responsibility for their own money, regardless of their income bracket.

Of course, you should continue to discover information from experts.

But the consciousness to learn and conquer the money demons has to come from within you. If you're sincere about educating yourself about personal finance, you won't be duped into paying lawyers and accountants to give you financial advice (that they may not even know themselves).

Average American Pays Higher Percentage In Taxes Than Billionaires

According to the latest data from the Bureau of Labor Statistics, the household income of an average American is $74,664, and they pay $10,489 in federal taxes, which is 14% of their average gross income.

Not to mention, they also bear the burden of paying state and local taxes; Social Security and Medicare taxes; vehicle and property taxes; and various other taxes.

However, the most famous name in the arena of investing, Warren Buffet, paid only 0.1% of his earnings in taxes (from 2014 to 2018) even though his wealth surged by 24.3 billion in those four years.

Jeff Bezos, whose wealth surged by $127 billion in a span of 20 years, paid only 1.1% of his income in taxes over that same period.[84]

So now you know the difference between the earnings of the rich and the average American, and also the difference in their tax payments. While billionaires are paying 0.1% to 1.1% of their colossal earnings, the average professional is paying 14% of their much smaller income.[91]

If you're wondering how that is even possible, you need to pay heed to the strategies they use, which we covered in this book.

The wealthiest individuals understand that they have the power to compound their wealth by using debt wisely, acquiring/building assets, and saving on taxes. There's no reason you shouldn't follow their example.

TURN THE HOUSE'S EDGE IN YOUR FAVOR

This is exactly how you begin to turn the "house's edge" in your favor. Understanding and implementing the "Buy, Borrow, and Die" strategy is the ideal way to conquer all three pitfalls in one fell swoop:

- You'll turn "mindless debt" into "strategic debt",
- You'll avoid taxes by leveraging assets, and
- You'll beat inflation by increasing your purchasing power while amplifying your net worth.

CONCLUSION

Congratulations! You now have everything you need to defeat the money villains, win the money game and become a financial wizard.

Now that we've come to the end, let's recap what we've covered. We can break down the G.A. Money System into six simple steps.

First, you must get acquainted with the playing field of money to win the game. The better you know the rules of the game and the financial pitfalls, the easier you will recognize opportunities you would have been blind to before.

Second, develop the habit of saving. Remember Arkad's lesson, "A part of all you earn is yours to keep." As you develop this mentality, you will become enthusiastic about the money you are setting aside. Within a short time, you will have amassed a sum of money you can be proud of.

Third, eliminate unnecessary debt. This will free up your mental energy around money and allow you to defeat the first money villain. Consider debt repayment strategies like the avalanche and snowball methods. Be more selective about your spending habits.

Fourth, you must lower your tax burden. If you aren't aware of the tax benefits you can avail yourself of, you could pay 50% in taxes in certain situations. The higher the income you make, the higher the tax amount you'll be liable to pay, so you should try to save on taxes as much as possible. Otherwise, you will lose $0.44 of every dollar to the government.

Fifth, put your money in places that have the chance to keep up with inflation. What works best is to seek appreciating (income-producing) assets that provide stable returns. Realize when you are investing money, there is always the chance of loss.

Sixth, while debt is commonly considered to be evil, it can be a clever way of growing your wealth. Thus, you must learn to borrow money strategically. This is not the same as borrowing money to put diamonds in your dentures. This is about borrowing money with a strategy to put the money to use to acquire more income-producing assets. This strategy is known as "Buy, Borrow, Die", and avoids taxes while beating inflation simultaneously, when done properly.

As a reminder, this book is not meant to tell you an exact step-by-step of what to do to be financially independent because each situation is different. For multiple reasons, what will work for you, may not work for someone else, and vice versa.

Your financial practices need to be tied to your priorities and preferences. However, the foundation of exceptional personal finance habits is the same for everyone.

No matter where you're at in life right now, you need to educate yourself financially. The earlier you do it, the better it is for you.

A critical time to educate yourself financially is when you're still in high school or college, and have plenty of time to bounce back from financial mishaps.

This book aims to give you specific knowledge about money, allowing you to set yourself apart from the masses and achieve financial freedom. Schools worldwide have been failing to teach us this information for generations.

With this information, you now know more about how to play the game of money than 99% of the people you know. It doesn't mean the game is 'easy' to play. It simply means you (finally) see the game.

Now you can do the proper research and take specific steps to get better at the money game over time.

For more information, subscribe to my newsletter as I give personal testimonies from my life and exclusive bonuses, including an extensive list of money secrets you can use to jumpstart your next steps:

Visit www.101MoneySecrets.com to get instant access.

If you found this book insightful and helpful, please share your feedback on Amazon so that other potential readers (and myself) can benefit from your unique perspective.

TO YOUR SUCCESS!!

A Gift To Our Readers

101+ Money Secrets that you can
download and put to use right away.
Visit this link:

www.101MoneySecrets.com

REFERENCES

1. *Throwback Thursday: How Much Have Housing Prices Risen Since 1950?* (2022, June 21). CMS Mortgage Solutions Inc. https://cmsmortgage. com/throwback-thursday-much-housing-prices-risen-since-1950/

2. US Census Bureau. (2021, October 8). *Income of Families and Persons in the United States: 1950.* Census.gov. https://www.census.gov/library/ publications/1952/demo/p60-009.html

3. Joy, C., PhD. (2021, December 16). *"Go to school, get a job, and you'll be happy," they said.* Medium. https://chasejoy.medium.com/go-to-school-get-a-job-and-youll-be-happy-they-said-47d0fe0a7a55

4. Inside Higher Ed. (2022, February 25). *Survey: College students need help with financial literacy.* https://www.insidehighered.com/news/ 2022/02/25/survey-college-students-need-help-financial-literacy

5. McGurran, B. (2022, March 28). *College Tuition Inflation: Compare The Cost Of College Over Time.* Forbes Advisor. https://www.forbes.com/ advisor/student-loans/college-tuition-inflation/

6. *A Look at the Shocking Student Loan Debt Statistics for 2021.* (2018). Student Loan Hero. https://studentloanhero.com/student-loan-debt-statistics/

7. Friedman, Z. (2018, June 13). *Student Loan Debt Statistics In 2018: A $1.5 Trillion Crisis.* Forbes. https://www.forbes.com/sites/ zackfriedman/2018/06/13/student-loan-debt-statistics-2018/?sh= 739235797310

8. Norvilitis, J. M. (2002). *Credit card debt on college campuses: causes, consequences, and solutions.* https://www.researchgate.net/profile/Jill-Norvilitis-2/publication/237462075_Credit_card_debt_on_college_ campuses_causes_consequences_and_solutions/links/ 0046353187b6115cdc000000/Credit-card-debt-on-college-campuses-causes-consequences-and-solutions.pdf

9. Matherne, C. (2021, December 14). *College Student Credit Card Debt.* WalletHub. https://wallethub.com/answers/cc/average-credit-card-debt-for-college-students-2140670817/

10. Brown, L. (2021, September 1). *Student Money Survey 2021 – Results.* Save the Student. https://www.savethestudent.org/money/surveys/student-money-survey-2021-results.html

11. Johnson, A. (2022, February 8). *Poll: Only Half Of Americans Have More Emergency Savings Than Credit Card Debt.* Bankrate. https://www.bankrate.com/personal-finance/debt/credit-card-debt-emergency-savings-2022/

12. Digangi, C. (2017, March 22). *Americans are dying with an average of $62,000 of debt.* Blog.credit.com. https://www.cbsnews.com/news/americans-are-dying-with-an-average-of-62k-of-debt/

13. Fram, A. (2011, April 5). *Poll reveals baby boomers' retirement fears.* NBC News. https://www.nbcnews.com/id/wbna42436897

14. Jenkin, T. (2016, January 6). *The Greatest Fear In Life: Dying or Running Out Of Money?* OXYGen Financial. https://oxygenfinancial.com/blog/the-greatest-fear-in-life-dying-or-running-out-of-money

15. Pastor, C. C. (2022, June 7). *2 Reasons Companies Don't Offer Pensions Anymore.* The Motley Fool. https://www.fool.com/the-ascent/buying-stocks/articles/2-reasons-companies-dont-offer-pensions-anymore/

16. Fontinelle, A. (2022, April 24). *The Biggest Financial Hurdles Young People Face.* Investopedia. https://www.investopedia.com/financial-edge/0712/the-biggest-financial-hurdles-young-people-face.aspx

17. Pye, J. (2022, October 3). *15 Celebrities You'd Never Guess Were in Debt.* Debt.com. https://www.debt.com/news/celebrities-youd-never-guess-were-in-debt/

18. *IRS provides tax inflation adjustments for tax year 2022* | Internal Revenue Service. (2021, November 10). IRS.gov. https://www.irs.gov/newsroom/irs-provides-tax-inflation-adjustments-for-tax-year-2022

19. Olya, G. (2020, February 6). *Pro Athletes Who Have Lost Millions of Dollars*. GOBankingRates. https://www.gobankingrates.com/net-worth/sports/pro-athletes-lost-millions-dollars/

20. Butler, N. (2015, August 19). *Percent of Your Income is Going to Taxes*. Paradigmlife.net Blog. https://paradigmlife.net/blog/what-percent-of-your-income-goes-to-all-types-of-tax/

21. Osterland, A. (2021, January 11). *State tax departments set their sights on pro athletes' earnings*. CNBC. https://www.cnbc.com/2021/01/11/state-tax-departments-set-their-sights-on-pro-athletes-earnings-.html

22. Santana, J. (2022, February 4). *What is the Jock Tax? A Guide for Athletes*. AWM Capital. https://awmcap.com/blog/jock-tax-2020

23. Patterson, E. (2015, December 16). *How Many Different Taxes Do We Pay? Here's the answer*. Paradigmlife.net Blog. https://paradigmlife.net/blog/ready-to-get-depressed-how-many-different-taxes-do-i-pay/

24. *History of Federal Income Tax Rates: 1913 – 2019*. (2019). Bradfordtaxinstitute. https://bradfordtaxinstitute.com/Free_Resources/Federal-Income-Tax-Rates.aspx

25. *78% of employees live paycheck to paycheck*. (2019, November 25). HEC Paris. https://www.hec.edu/en/news-room/78-employees-live-paycheck-paycheck

26. Today, P. (n.d.). Accessed October 28, 2022. *Mental well-being inherently connected to financial wellness*. Purdue University News. https://www.purdue.edu/newsroom/purduetoday/releases/2021/Q1/mental-well-being-inherently-connected-to-financial-wellness.html

27. Schwahn, L. (2021, December 7). *How Much Money Should I Save Each Month?* NerdWallet. https://www.nerdwallet.com/article/finance/how-much-should-i-save-each-month

28. *How much do I need to retire?* | Fidelity. (2021, August 27). Fidelity. https://www.fidelity.com/viewpoints/retirement/how-much-do-i-need-to-retire

29. Pant, P. (2021, December 29). *The Incredible Power of Saving 50 Percent of Your Income.* The Balance. https://www.thebalance.com/the-incredible-power-of-saving-50-percent-453969

30. *7 Compelling Reasons to Encourage Your Teen to Save Money, Starting Today.* (n.d.). Studentsuper.com.au. https://www.studentsuper.com.au/blog/7-compelling-reasons-to-encourage-your-teen-to-save-money-starting-today/

31. *Better Money Habits® 2020 Millennial Report.* (n.d.). Bank of America. Retrieved September 15, 2022, from https://about.bankofamerica.com/en/making-an-impact/bmh-millennial-report?cm_mmc=EBZ-EnterpriseBrand-_-vanity-_-EB01VN00GZ_millennialreport-_-N/

32. Moore, K. (2020, June 3). *Why Saving Isn't Enough.* Finivi. https://www.finivi.com/why-saving-isnt-enough/

33. *U.S. All Grades All Formulations Retail Gasoline Prices (Dollars per Gallon).* (2010). Eia.gov. https://www.eia.gov/dnav/pet/hist/LeafHandler.ashx?n=PET&s=EMM_EPM0_PTE_NUS_DPG&f=A

34. Domm, P. (2022, June 11). *Gasoline prices top $5 a gallon nationally for the first time and are likely headed higher.* CNBC. https://www.cnbc.com/2022/06/11/gasoline-prices-top-5-a-gallon-nationally-for-the-first-time-and-are-likely-headed-higher.html

35. *US Average Household Income by Year.* (n.d.). multpl. https://www.multpl.com/us-average-income/table/by-year

36. Morrow, A. (2022, April 18). *Inflation, explained: Why prices keep going up and who's to blame.* CNN. https://edition.cnn.com/2022/01/09/economy/what-is-inflation-and-whos-to-blame/index.html

37. Nunley, J. (2022, June 3). *Why are prices going up?* UW-La Crosse. https://www.uwlax.edu/currents/why-are-prices-going-up/

38. Hayes, A. (2022, May 27). *Purchasing Power Definition.* Investopedia. https://www.investopedia.com/terms/p/purchasingpower.asp

39. Kenton, W. (2022, May 31). *Understanding the Rule of 72.* Investopedia. https://www.investopedia.com/terms/r/ruleof72.asp

40. Beniwal, H. (2012, October 31). *Rule of 72 & Super Mario Personal Finance Lessons*. The Financial Literates. https://www.tflguide.com/rule-of-72/

41. *US Inflation Rate Rises above Forecasts in March*. (2021, April 10). Trading Economics. https://tradingeconomics.com/united-states/inflation-cpi

42. *Investing Long Term? Don't Overlook the Inflation Factor!* (n.d.). www.tdbank.com. https://www.tdbank.com/personal/investment-resources/articles/article-InvestingLongTerm.html

43. Nick Bollettieri. (2017, December 20). *#AskNick: What do you see when you look in the mirror?* Tennis. https://www.tennis.com/news/articles/asknick-what-do-you-see-when-you-look-in-the-mirror

44. Blowers, D. (2019, March 24). *Acing the Basics: Why Fundamentals Are Everything*. The Post-Grad Survival Guide. https://medium.com/the-post-grad-survival-guide/acing-the-basics-why-fundamentals-are-everything-c20855c65b41

45. *Basketball Drills for Beginners - Basic Fundamentals for Kids*. (2015). Online Basketball Drills. https://www.online-basketball-drills.com/basketball-drills/beginners

46. H. Kent Baker, Nofsinger, J. R., & Vesa Puttonen. (2020). *The savvy investor's guide to avoiding pitfalls, frauds, and scams*. Emerald Publishing.

47. Mayrath, N. (2019, January 5). *Confessions of a broke financial advisor*. Yahoo. https://www.yahoo.com/now/confessions-broke-financial-advisor-213008745.html

48. *What does it mean when your financial advisor files for bankruptcy?* (2017, March 8). The White Law Group. https://www.whitesecuritieslaw.com/financial-advisor-files-bankruptcy/

49. Skinner, L. (2014, June 6). *How advisers bounce back from bankruptcy*. InvestmentNews. https://www.investmentnews.com/how-advisers-bounce-back-from-bankruptcy-57972

50. Statista. (2022, October 19). *U.S. number of personal bankruptcy filings nationwide 2000-2021.* https://www.statista.com/statistics/817911/number-of-non-business-bankruptcies-in-the-united-states/

51. Neiger, C. (2020, October 28). *Casino Stats: Why Gamblers Rarely Win.* Investopedia. https://www.investopedia.com/financial-edge/0910/casino-stats-why-gamblers-rarely-win.aspx

52. *Advantage play in blackjack.* (n.d.). Accessed October 28, 2022. Gambling Sites; GamblingSites.org. https://www.gamblingsites.org/casino/blackjack/advantage-play/

53. Curnow, D. (2020, March 25). *How to Become a Professional Blackjack Player: Tips and a Short Guide.* Pokernews.com. https://www.pokernews.com/casino/professional-blackjack-player-guide.htm

54. Rose, J. (2019, September 9). *GF¢ 029: 7 Financial Advisors I Would Like to Punch in the Face.* Good Financial Cents®. https://www.goodfinancialcents.com/7-financial-advisors-i-would-like-to-punch-in-the-face/

55. William, H. (1993, June). *A financial planner = good communication skills. (Personal Financial Planning).* Archives.cpajournal.com. http://archives.cpajournal.com/old/14465881.htm

56. Jones, C. (2020, March 2). *Confessions of A Retired Investment Advisor and Financial Planner.* Clifford Jones - Strategic Business Advisor Helping Business Leaders Go to Market with Clarity and Confidence. https://cliffordjones.com/2020/03/confessions-of-a-retired-investment-advisor-and-financial-planner/

57. Claessens, S., & Laeven, L. (2004). *Competition in the Financial Sector and Growth: A Cross-Country Perspective.* Financial Development and Economic Growth, 66–105. https://doi.org/10.1057/9780230374270_3

58. Wack, K. (2020, August 28). *Ex-Bank of America employees allege "extreme pressure" to sell credit cards.* American Banker. https://www.americanbanker.com/news/ex-bank-of-america-employees-allege-extreme-pressure-to-sell-credit-cards

59. *These Are the Most Hated Banks in Every U.S. State.* (2020, August 10). FairShake. https://fairshake.com/consumer-guides/most-hated-banks-us/

60. Rupe, S. (2018, October 18). *Consumers "More Confused Than Ever" By Financial Planning.* InsuranceNewsNet. https://insurancenewsnet. com/innarticle/consumers-more-confused-than-ever-by-financial-planning

61. Sherter, A. (2011, April 5). *Read It and Weep: Why Financial Literacy is a Crock.* Cbsnews.com. https://www.cbsnews.com/news/read-it-and-weep-why-financial-literacy-is-a-crock/

62. Snyder, K. (2022, April 5). *The Richest Man in Babylon Summary.* Clever Girl Finance. https://www.clevergirlfinance.com/blog/the-richest-man-in-babylon-summary/

63. Anderson, P. (2011, September 12). *Save And Pay Yourself First: A Part Of All I Earned Was Mine To Keep.* Bible Money Matters. https://www. biblemoneymatters.com/save-and-pay-yourself-first-a-part-of-all-i-earned-was-mine-to-keep/

64. *How to Build an Emergency Fund.* (2022, June 30). Investopedia. https://www.investopedia.com/personal-finance/how-to-build-emergency-fund/

65. *Bank mistakenly puts $37 million in Texas woman's account.* (2019, December 13). ABC7 Chicago. https://abc7chicago.com/millionaire-bank-mix-up-woman-gets-millions-in-account-accidentally-puts-womans/5751474/

66. Egan, J. (2022, June 8). *How To Get Out of Credit Card Debt in 7 Steps.* Credit Karma. https://www.creditkarma.com/advice/i/how-to-get-out-of-credit-card-debt

67. *Tips to Pay Off Credit Card Debt Fast.* (n.d.). Accessed October 28, 2022. Better Money Habits. https://bettermoneyhabits. bankofamerica.com/en/debt/how-to-pay-off-credit-card-debt-fast

68. Underwood, J. (2021, January 1). *How To Use Your Credit Card Grace Period To Avoid Paying Interest.* Forbes Advisor. https://www.forbes.

com/advisor/credit-cards/how-to-use-your-credit-card-grace-period-to-avoid-paying-interest/

69. LaPonsie, M. (2022, January 27). *15 Legal Secrets to Reducing Your Taxes. US News & World Report; U.S. News & World Report.* Money.Usnews. https://money.usnews.com/money/personal-finance/articles/legal-secrets-to-reducing-your-taxes

70. Rae, D. (2022, April 22). *11 Tax Deductions To Help Small Business Owners Minimize Their Taxes.* Forbes. https://www.forbes.com/sites/davidrae/2022/04/12/11-tax-deductions-to-help-small-business-owners-minimize-their-taxes/?sh=4c3c6d513d30

71. *How do the rich avoid taxes by starting their own 501(c)(3)?* (n.d.). Quora. Retrieved August 22, 2022, from https://www.quora.com/How-do-the-rich-avoid-taxes-by-starting-their-own-501-c-3

72. *Guide to Tax Deductions for Nonprofit Organizations.* (2020, November 30). FreshBooks. https://www.freshbooks.com/hub/taxes/nonprofit-tax-deductions-for-501c3-organizations

73. *Can You Get Rich Running A Charity?* (2012, November 6). Charity Navigator. https://www.charitynavigator.org/index.cfm?bay=content.view&cpid=1458

74. Segal, T. (2022, March 29). *Can IRAs Reduce Your Taxable Income?* Investopedia. https://www.investopedia.com/ask/answers/102714/do-ira-contributions-reduce-average-gross-income-agi.asp

75. Murphy, A., & Contreras, I. (Eds.). (2022, May 12). *The Global 2000 2022.* Forbes. https://www.forbes.com/lists/global2000/?sh=410b3ada5ac0

76. Hanson, C. (2017, September 25). *Leverage Your Money Like a Bank!* Paradigmlife.net Blog. https://paradigmlife.net/blog/leverage-money-like-bank/

77. Money, P. (2013, April 2). *Is It True That Savers Are the Banks' Creditors?* Positive Money. https://positivemoney.org/2013/04/is-it-true-that-savers-are-the-banks-creditors/

78. Kagan, J. (2022, August 10). *Fractional Reserve Banking*. Investopedia. https://www.investopedia.com/terms/f/fractionalreservebanking.asp

79. Dautovic, G. (2022, January 19). *Where Do Banks Get Money to Lend to Borrowers?* Fortunly. https://fortunly.com/articles/where-do-banks-get-money-to-lend-to-borrowers/#gref

80. Chen, J. (2020, October 10). *Yield Spread: Definition, How It Works, and Types of Spreads*. Investopedia. https://www.investopedia.com/terms/y/yieldspread.asp

81. Gravier, E. (2021, June 25). *Here's where experts recommend you should put your money during an inflation surge*. CNBC. https://www.cnbc.com/select/where-to-put-your-money-during-inflation-surge/

82. Gupta, A. (2020, October 4). *Understanding Infinite Banking and how to be your own bank*. The making of a millionaire. https://themakingofamillionaire.com/understanding-infinite-banking-and-how-to-be-your-own-bank-66668849aa8c

83. Kredell, M. (2021, August 30). *"Buy, borrow, die" gains new life*. Gould.usc.edu. https://gould.usc.edu/about/news/?id=4887

84. Eisinger, J., Ernsthausen, J., & Kiel, P. (2021, June 8). *The Secret IRS Files: Trove of Never-Before-Seen Records Reveal How the Wealthiest Avoid Income Tax*. ProPublica. https://www.propublica.org/article/the-secret-irs-files-trove-of-never-before-seen-records-reveal-how-the-wealthiest-avoid-income-tax

85. Ensign, R. L., & Rubin, R. (2021, July 13). *Buy, Borrow, Die: How Rich Americans Live Off Their Paper Wealth*. WSJ. https://www.wsj.com/articles/buy-borrow-die-how-rich-americans-live-off-their-paper-wealth-11625909583

86. Hyatt, J. (2021, November 11). *How America's Richest People Can Access Billions Without Selling Their Stock*. Forbes. https://www.forbes.com/sites/johnhyatt/2021/11/11/how-americas-richest-people-larry-ellison-elon-musk-can-access-billions-without-selling-their-stock/?sh=3fc4be6d23d4

87. Bhutada, G. (2021, April 6). *Purchasing Power of the U.S. Dollar Over Time*. Visual Capitalist. https://www.visualcapitalist.com/ purchasing-power-of-the-u-s-dollar-over-time/

88. Barnes, J. (n.d.). Accessed October 28, 2022. *What is OPM?* REtipster. https://retipster.com/terms/opm/

89. *Deferred Payment Fix and Flip Loan*. (2018, January 17). FBC Funding. https://www.rehablender.net/deferred-payment-fix-and-flip-loan/

90. Farrington, R. (2021, September 13). *How Ordinary Americans Can Also Buy, Borrow, And Die Without Paying Taxes*. Forbes. https://www. forbes.com/sites/robertfarrington/2021/09/13/how-ordinary-americans-can-also-buy-borrow-and-die-without-paying-taxes/? sh=741812dc124e

91. Frankel, M. (2018, April 22). *How Much Does the Average American Pay in Taxes?* The Motley Fool. https://www.fool.com/taxes/2018/04/22/ how-much-does-the-average-american-pay-in-taxes.aspx

IMAGE CREDITS

Akyurt, E. (2021). *HD photo by engin akyurt* [Image]. Unsplash. https://unsplash.com/photos/CTsI2OuMYaM

Barbhuiya, T. (2021a). *Person holding brown leather bifold wallet* [Image]. Unsplash. https://unsplash.com/photos/3aGZ7a97qwA

Barbhuiya, T. (2021b). *Free plant image* [Image]. Unsplash. https://unsplash.com/photos/joqWSI9u_XM

Barbhuiya, T. (2021c). *HD photo by Towfiqu barbhuiya* [Image]. Unsplash. https://unsplash.com/photos/M8z2SwSwpbg

Busch, F. (2019). *Man wearing white top looking at projector graph screen* [Image]. Unsplash. https://unsplash.com/photos/PzifgmBsxCc

CA, P. (2019a). *Investment scrabble text photo* [Image]. Unsplash. https://unsplash.com/photos/OlSGcrLSYkw

CA, P. (2019b). *Mortgage scrabble tiles* [Image]. Unsplash. https://unsplash.com/photos/uJ7NOEbTd80

Dawson, S. (2018). *Turned on monitoring screen* [Image]. Unsplash. https://unsplash.com/photos/qwtCeJ5cLYs

DeLawrence, O. (2020). *Black and silver pen on white paper* [Image]. Unsplash. https://unsplash.com/photos/5616whx5NdQ

Eliason, K. (2017). *1 U.S. dollar banknote* [Image]. Unsplash. https://unsplash.com/photos/8fDhgAN5zG0

Evans, A. (2020). *White and blue magnetic card* [Image]. Unsplash. https://unsplash.com/photos/RJQE64NmC_o

GoodNotes. (2022). *HD photo by GoodNotes* [Image]. Unsplash. https://unsplash.com/photos/1s5TOXcMZQ8

Hall, N. (2021). *Woman in white long sleeve shirt holding white printer paper* [Image]. Unsplash. https://unsplash.com/photos/o8KUqjk9gqE

Hunter, A. (2018). *Woman standing at front of concrete fence wearing academic uniform* [Image]. Unsplash. https://unsplash.com/photos/AQ908FfdAMw

Martin, E. (2017). *Grey concrete building* [Image]. Unsplash. https://unsplash.com/photos/2_K82gx9Uk8

Pan, J. (2021). *Gold and black metal tool* [Image]. Unsplash. https://unsplash.com/photos/iYsrkq5qq0Q

regularguy.eth. (2021). *Free losing money* [Image]. Unsplash. https://unsplash.com/photos/K_3UV1ZFcJ0

Stojanovski, P. (2018). *Closeup photo of 100 US dollar banknotes* [Image]. Unsplash. https://unsplash.com/photos/MJSFNZ8BAXw

Taissin, A. (2020). *Pink pig coin bank on brown wooden table* [Image]. Unsplash. https://unsplash.com/photos/5OUMf1Mr5pU

Weerasinghe, J. (2021). *Silver and black round emblem* [Image]. Unsplash. https://unsplash.com/photos/NHRM1u4GD_A